Also By Tevin Curtis Ryan Dubé

Book Of The Enlightened One

Amen: A Great Light Within Divine Darkness

The Mystery Behind Life, Death and Resurrection

A
Silent Truth

Tevin C. R. Dubé

© 2018 Tevin Curtis Ryan Dubé. All rights reserved.

ISBN: 978-976-8280-41-1

Publishers Note

No part of this publication may be reproduced, stored in, or introduced into a retrieval system, or transmitted in any form or by means (electronic, mechanical, photocopying, recording, or otherwise) without prior consent of the copyright owner.

Tevin Curtis Ryan Dubé

Trinidad and Tobago

Email: tevindube@yahoo.com

FaceBook Page –Tevin 'Mystical' Dube

Instagram – mystical_dube

Twitter – @mysticaldube

Cover Design by Tevin C. R. Dubé

Cover Illustration by Kurt Hilton

Acknowledgement

To the Universal Most High Supreme Divine Being, my reverence towards Thee can be ineffable sometimes. My works are a result of that deep inward connection we both continuously establish and will eternally share.

This here is also attributed to my ancestors and the powerful lineages that flow through my veins. I will forever be humbled by an eternal imprint within my soul. It is the inheritance of a true Spiritual Nature that is ever of royalty and filled with all manner of mystical divinities.

I dedicate this to the future generation: Jahiem and Jaylon Dubé, Kwasi Kael Dubé Jr. and Kymani Dubé, Arianna and Aiden Dubé, to a very special Denzayah Harricharan whose birth marks the same day in which both my father and his grandmother had transitioned from this life, Jayden Telesford, Darieem Teesdale, Joseph, Faith and Levi Andrews, Nikkel Collymore, Cody and Kayla Wells, Abigail Duntin, Brittney, Brianna and Jayshawn Blackwell.

To Makhaya Legendre, a youth with who I can identify many great characteristics, which I too, naturally possessed as a child, Kieron Legendre, Kershiah Edwards and Stephon Burton, Alyssa Collymore, Dylandre Wellington and to another special child called Zendeya Babatunde whose birth I predicted about 5 months in advance. Today we both share the same birthday.

I want to extend sincere appreciation to my mother KathyAnn Marie Toppin, and my brothers, Nigel Telesford, Keion Collymore, Clinton Legendre and Martina Loubon-Legendre.

I want to make special mention of Denneisha O'Garro and Christabell Renee Seeparsad for your kind words and support when it was needed most. To all those who genuinely support me, I truly appreciate every one of you.

Author's Note

The true beauty of this book in particular came as a result of a pure form of inspiration. The honey within came to me when my mind was free from all thoughts.

I began to record my everyday thoughts as I remained in solitude for some time. Using my WhatsApp status as my immediate writing grounds, I documented and screenshot these free thoughts. The text layout was patterned after a similar format.

These poems/inspirational quotes are very deep and relatable as they portray the depths of many thoughts that were involuntarily conceived, decoded and then voluntarily recorded. It is also a one-to-one conversation with my subconscious mind that is always vocal but is yet to be heard.

It is also a documentation of my many emotions as I journey through this newfound life of mine. Therefore, you will come across my many silent battles, betrayal, envy and jealousy, fight downs, profound realisations, wins and losses and so much more as I continue to try to establish myself after already publishing three books.

This is only the prelude leading up to the story of life my life. Everything will all make sense in time.

Tevin C. R. Dubé

Let us enter

into a Universal

Mind that is a

Mind Universal.

When you have learned to see that all of your blessings are curses and all of your curses are blessings, it is at that moment you become a full circle with Life itself.

Some people

has to be

blinded, in order to see.

A Silent Truth

Life is made perfect through imperfections. In other words, by learning from our mistakes we are perfected. I don't expect you to be perfect when I already know that you are. I want nothing else from you other than you being you.

Tevin C. R. Dubé

Sometimes I can't make sense or trace my life's purpose. At those moments I acknowledge my temporary blindness, calm my mind and walk with an optimistic faith. It is all an illusion to make you lose focus and fight against yourself.

A Silent Truth

ll I had was a broken heart and a shattered dream. So then I asked the question, what this Life has for me? As I broke myself down, something mysterious was rebuilding me. And now I am reborn into a new being.

Tevin C. R. Dubé

I just want someone to be real with me. Come with your insecurities and fears and we will both learn to deal with it all together.

ut of the 3.96 billion women on planet Earth, I only saw you recently. I've seen the woman of my dreams in a dream.

Tevin C. R. Dubé

I magine

loneliness was

tired of seeing

me lonely, so it

decided to

leave me

alone.

A Silent Truth

As I do often repeat, "I Am Not Perfect." It is just that I was given a tiny purpose by the Most High Divine and through me, many things are perfected. I am human just as much as you, making mistakes, have regrets, been broken, does cry a little but still dust myself off and try my best to be better each day. I try to show love in every possible way, be encouraging and motivating. It's exhausting but somebody has to do it and I guess it's a lucky number Tevin.

Tevin C. R. Dubé

There is a

great

difference

between

achievements

and

accomplishments.

A Silent Truth

If I ever tell you that I love you, trust me, I really do mean it because such words rarely leaves my mouth. I'll more prove it in my simplest ways but if I do say it to you, just know that it came from a place deep within my soul.

Tevin C. R. Dubé

Everyone may know that neither of us are perfect but as soon as one makes a mistake, many start suffering from amnesia by turning around with pointed fingers to judge you for not being perfect.

A Silent Truth

Some people are afraid to sleep because of nightmares whereas some are afraid of the day because they are living out their fears.

Tevin C. R. Dubé

My gas tank is currently in reserved but yet still I'm covering miles of travel as an aeroplane. Supernatural fuel!

A Silent Truth

Everything has a season. When it's my time to be rewarded for my labours, make sure to never measure my pay without knowing the nature of my task. Never see my glory without knowing my story. Don't only see my blessings by trying to understand my curses. Then you would fully understand me. And after such, I'll be more than willing to share my wealth with you.

Tevin C. R. Dubé

I am still grateful through it all; the highs and lows, the ups and downs, joy and sorrow, thick and thin. Only the Lord knows the weight to bear, so I'm grateful for the strength given. It is no an easy task to change the world but yet still one man can do it by simply reinventing one mind at a time.

ll the people

who are trying

to keep you

down are

already lying

down. Keep

standing tall.

Some people choose to sit in Life while others choose to stand tall. You are the result of your choices because the choice has always been you.

Folklore creatures that suck you dry:

1. Vampires
2. Dementors (Harry Potter)
3. Soucouyant (Trinidad and Tobago obeah tales)

In reality:

1. Negative people
2. Ungrateful people
3. Fake people

In Trinidad, you can find at least 4.

Tevin C. R. Dubé

When you are

daily surrounded

by negativity,

remain positive.

They may act

like it but

without you, the

the battery will never work.

A Silent Truth

I claim to have solved a lifelong mystery. It was indeed hidden because it has been lifelong since I had been born. It was indeed a mystery because it wasn't my time to be revealed. The mystery had no choice but to be concealed because it could have only been revealed because of me. Only I could have transported it because the mystery was me all along.

Tevin C. R. Dubé

Most times when we upgrade from one state to another, we treat our new inheritance as something we could never live without. Remember Life is a a replay of events to be perfected.

Young grapes are always bitter but in time it is the sweetest. Allow yourself to be transformed beautifully. The same people who don't want you now will eventually see the need of you later. But not everyone would be able to afford the luxury of your presence.

Tevin C. R. Dubé

The greatest attribute you can have as an adult is to maintain a childlike innocence. This way, forgiveness and love comes easily and naturally.

A Silent Truth

My words are encrypted. It's like I feel everything at the same time. All my emotions are blended so I appear numb. I'll be happy and remember sadness is looking for companionship. It's exhausting to always be on your guard because Life is unpredictable but I guess this my burden to bear so I do try my best to uplift people but as I take on the burden of the world, I wonder who's praying for my soul.

Tevin C. R. Dubé

I never saw love as

an option in my life.

It's like I've been

there, done that

even though I've

never really been

there and done

that. But the future

from within my loins is

depending on me.

A Silent Truth

The reason why we suffer so much is because Life itself is sometimes jealous of its reflection called Death. We all want to live forever but in the end we still choose to die.

Tevin C. R. Dubé

I've got a water well in my mind, springing a lake divine. You could flip a penny and maybe then make a wish. Or if you wish to get clean, you're welcome to bathe, so feel free to take a dive in this. You can lead a horse to a lake but you could never make it drink. Remember ignorance is bliss; just follow your intuition because no mortal man could never outthink it.

A Silent Truth

At times I can't even begin to fathom what exactly it is that I have done to be uplifted in such mysterious ways. Maybe it's because of my selfless services no one sees. I will give my last without looking for anything in return. Maybe it's because my heart is ever filled with compassion. Maybe it's because my mind always emulates balanced thoughts towards all. Maybe it's because I demonstrate a genuine spirituality. All I can say is thank you Universal Divine Supreme.

Tevin C. R. Dubé

I have the power to create anything I desire. Everything I've done thus far is as a result of my imagination and sheer determination to accomplish it. Now you can bear witness that the Universe has given to me it's approval. Now I can place my signature to where it rightfully belongs.

A Silent Truth

Personally, I believe when nobody wants you, the more appealing you will become. And when you become this way, that's the time when you don't need anybody. The wait is hard and can at times seem to be unfair and messed up but hopefully, one day, you'll find everything you need more in that one special person whom was carefully crafted, designed and specifically tailored to suit you only.

Tevin C. R. Dubé

The moment I realized I truly

had nothing else left to give,

I began to give away my most

prized possession; my love.

Not everyone deserves it and surely

not everyone would truly appreciate

it. But the choice was mine to

share it even though many wouldn't

even spare a fraction of theirs

towards me. I suffered greatly

trying to be what I would

love others

to be unto me.

ow could you

truly out my

light now that

I've mastered having

clear vision in

the dark?

Tevin C. R. Dubé

I am so electronically charged that even my silent thoughts create a never-ending ripple throughout the entire Universe and Beyond. I have become the very droplet that can vibrate an entire Ocean at a simple touch.

A Silent Truth

You can feel the air without touching it. Now I know why I am able to influence your emotions without persuasively speaking to it. It's ironic that I made you fall in love with me even before you knew it.

Tevin C. R. Dubé

I t's all in your

eyes. Your lips

saying I'm shy

but your eyes,

are gladly inviting

me to come inside.

A Silent Truth

The energy you give to me is like peace amidst war. Your love centres my life and moves with me. You are the Eye of my Storm.

Tevin C. R. Dubé

I have become so accustomed to hearing the voice of a silent frequency emulating loudly from within me that it is easy for me to read people from time to time. I can tell when your energy is off, hear thoughts and sense people's intentions. It's tough for a mortal man without true understanding but this is when you are becoming in tune with yourself by becoming in sync with Nature. It is a Universal Language only a few can speak without saying a word.

 beautiful body will always attract lustful eyes and flattering lips but a beautiful soul will always attract a realness that lasts for a lifetime and beyond. Let's get to know each other inside-out and not outside-in.

Tevin C. R. Dubé

When someone like me who has been facing storms after storms and battles after battles begin to finally, inherit my blessings after blessings please don't be against my happiness in general. There was a time when I was looking for love but love had other plans for me instead. So if you see someone is beginning to be another reason why I started to smile more often or that I've finally inherited something magnificent, don't ever try to steal my joy. Always remember I paid the price to earn that shit. And maybe it was the Most High Divine who

A Silent Truth

pitied my downtrodden soul

because I too suffered greatly

in more ways than one

while I was executing my

divine duties just like

when Adam was without Eve.

Tevin C. R. Dubé

If Jacob had to work

14 years before he

could have married Rachel

the love of his life and

Joseph, an old widower

was given the virgin

Mary who was a 17

year old at the time to

be his wife, then I too

shall remain positive

and confident and

humble within myself

by trusting my instincts.

A Silent Truth

There are those persistent thorns in a garden, always trying its utmost best to stifle the growth of a fruit tree. The farmer abhors it by plucking and exterminating it. What makes you think that the Most High loves an unproductive, conniving, non-bearing individual who is ever persistent in trying their best to suppress and fight down the one who is toiling to bear good fruits from their hard labours? You too shall be uprooted in the process.

Tevin C. R. Dubé

Tell me how you would feel

when you keep giving

everything, especially mentally and

emotionally to always help

people and in the end, all you

inherit is their problems because

now you have to be the solution

to find a solution. And in the

end, you remain with nothing

and are left undone. Whenever

it comes to you, your stuff

always seems to be delayed.

People do say don't worry,

that's why your reward will be

greater in the end. But what reward!

By losing your sanity by stabilizing

A Silent Truth

others at the expense of your

mental well-being! I don't need to know

anyone's secrets but they flock to me

because I possess the inability to judge.

I keep giving people the things I

could NEVER regain. My happiness! The

more I make them smile; they know

not how slowly I'm dying inside because

none is there for me when I'm in

need. My silence is strength

nevertheless. I'll no longer expose

my weakness because the fakes are

well concealed. As for my reward,

I'm sure many are thinking about

money. I don't need them shallow-

minded simpleton thinkers around me.

Tevin C. R. Dubé

I'm running out of options. What more can I do? Now would be a great time for a sign or some sort of revelation. I need it.

A Silent Truth

When I ask for something I do get it. I have a great opportunity that presented itself to me, only today. I am going fully prepared to capitalize on this occasion. Thanks for the sign dear Universal Supreme. Honestly, I am slowly becoming weary but I'm humbled every step of the way but we both know that I deserve my fair chance to receive all the great things that is long overdue unto me.

Tevin C. R. Dubé

When you awake from a sleeping race, it is hard trying to show someone else who is sound asleep how much of a comatose state they are within.

Feeling like Superman in the Null Void.

Tevin C. R. Dubé

Some people

hate to love

and some love

to hate.

A Silent Truth

I keep seeing all the

people who creating

grievances with me

are being blinded

and led to their

own demise by

the Great Divine

who lifted me up

from within the

stomach of Death

itself.

Tevin C. R. Dubé

To all the people who are talking behind my back I want to let you know that it is easier for you to kiss my ass.

A Silent Truth

It is necessary to do self-reflection often, if not daily. Correct and re-correct yourself under much scrutiny when it is in direct correlation to your thoughts, words and deeds. After such, you shall always seem to be exempted from harsh judgments universally. Humility will always triumph over self-righteousness.

My eyes are opened
and I've seen the
whole truth. The
time has come for
me to make a major
decision never to
hurt me again.
They all will forsake
you in the end.
2:18 am

A Silent Truth

I guess all this unhappiness is preparation for the the abundance of joy to come. I guess it is set to teach how to treasure it when it finally arrives. The only question is, how much longer must I endure? I know that it is coming, I just hope that I'm alive for it.

Tevin C. R. Dubé

I love the naysayers, doubters
and everyone else who is quick
to say you would never make it as
if it is they who had established the
sun and the moon. That is fuel to
my flames of passion. It ignites
my ego as it proves that I'm on
track with my destiny. My
humility will never allow vaunting
and this would always stir
bitterness in their hearts. But
utilizing a good ego will give you
the sweetest satisfaction when
you begin to defy all odds and break every
expectation and prove the
exact opposite. All heads shall
bow and every tongue shall confess.
Even if silently, You are the best!

I don't go into

the world looking

for friends. I go

into the world

looking to be

a friend.

Tevin C. R. Dubé

Some of us are blessed to have a healthy body and still complain. Some of us have a family and still complain. Some of us are wealthy and still complain. Some of us have somebody to love and still complain. The problem is that many of us are unable to see what we have so we complain. Others look on and pray to have what someone else has and most of us would never truly understand the pains of each wishing to be like the other. Some with good health are lonely. Some the families are not wealthy. Some who are wealthy are unhappy. The complications of Life are many and the blessings are disguised but do we truly have the overstanding to figure it all out?

The greatest lessons in Life are solely taught through pain and hurt.

Tevin C. R. Dubé

The greatest saints in Life were never saints.

A Silent Truth

The greatest form of meditation is the one when you can keep calm the mind during the constant motions of Life.

If you don't learn

how to master

your fears it reflects

upon your life

as you project it upon

those around

you.

To become bored

is to lack creativity.

To lack creativity

is to ineffectively

utilize the powers

of imagination.

Tevin C. R. Dubé

There are three

steps in the

Creation

Process:

1) Imagination

2) Belief

3) Work

A Silent Truth

The quickest and the easiest way to end your life is achieved through the process of procrastination.

Tevin C. R. Dubé

Remember gold was always valuable long before it was even discovered.

A Silent Truth

There are those
moments when I feel
like God in the flesh
but then I filled myself
with such pure humility
to never allow my ego
to be in control.
That part of me doesn't
belong within the realm
of physicality.

If you want to come to know more about the Divine Creator you have to go within your own soul and come to know more about Self.

A Silent Truth

It has been a pleasure getting to know you. Our relationship has been a journey thus far. What a constant learning experience it has been. Through the highs and the lows, you never left my side. I thank you for sticking it out with me, even when I wanted to leave. You showed me the strength I never knew I had. All I have is you, all I have is myself.

Tevin C. R. Dubé

Bury gold and still it would never lose its value, it would be all the more be in search of. Cover it with filth and yet still the lustre of it could never be tarnished. Pass it through fire and watch it becomes purified of all impurities. Be like gold my friend.

A Silent Truth

The same way a the banana tree already has every sucker plant within and every sucker the plant already has all the leaves folded within to last its entire lifespan, it is in the same manner that all the truth in which you are searching for are already to be had and more within you.

My tears are very precious because out from the intangible nature of an emotion, it bubbles naturally to the surface as a spring.

A Silent Truth

The sweat upon my skin is a natural mystic because it is the microcosm of that of the precipitation process occurring on a molecular level. Therefore, the clouds are not the only thing that rains but so too do my skin.

Change comes in the most unpredictable manner. It would start as a rain drop that contains the hidden potential of an entire ocean.

What comes first, the chicken or the egg? Or maybe the seed is as a result of the tree as much as the tree was first within the seed. Or is the ocean is as a result of many droplets as much as the ocean is within the containment of a single droplet. Questions left unanswered except for one possible scenario. Existence! Without it, 'Nothing' itself would have been possible to even exist.

Tevin C. R. Dubé

Change is like
growing hair or
a flower that
bloomed
overnight. You
may never truly
see it happening
until it happens.

The greatest source of inspiration comes from the purity of a mind that is free from all thoughts.

 graduation is to mark a successful completion. Death is nothing to be feared because to an enlightened mind it is the greatest accomplishment. It is the initiation and graduation from one level unto the attainment of newer heights.

A Silent Truth

Life is a humbling experience that is still frustrating to a Great Being who knows and has mastered the ability to fly but must now develop the true character that is demanded on foot.

Tevin C. R. Dubé

A broken spirit and contrite heart are the best offerings. Well, I've already given that and more. I have nothing left to offer, what more shall I do, what more shall I give? My eyes are exhausted with grief, my heart overwhelmed with pain; my spirit burdened and heavy. What more is required of me? My blood clot is within me, my oxygen level is now deplorable and my strength is depleting rapidly. A lonely sheep wandering the wilderness crying out to a shepherd who had already abandoned him long ago; a lonely sheep who must first die of its inward fear of being slaughtered by the ravenous predators that prey upon him. Was the sheep losing its way from the shepherd a good thing? The shepherd was rearing him to be slaughtered by his very own hands.

A Silent Truth

When you're down and out on your last, such a situation will open up your eyes to reveal the ugliness within many who keep preaching that they will never leave you. Haven't I seen enough? Haven't I already learnt this lesson time and again? What more is required of me? I have no one to turn to. In a world filled with people, am I to always be alone? The grave is already a lonely place, must I feel alone all my days until I reach that forsaken place?

Tevin C. R. Dubé

The thinks I have been through, the things I had to endure, the many terrifying experiences I had to confront, many would have been deceased by now.

This thing is getting one-sided and I can't even lie to me no more. Fix the entire world and remain broken in the end as a reward for your efforts.

Tevin C. R. Dubé

fter you have read the final chapter and the book has closed and the details of the story is slowly forgotten. It is the morals and concepts that remain without an end.

A Silent Truth

To all those who choose to willfully strive against me, I don't wish you bad. I pray you have to go through everything I've been through good and bad in every aspect. If you make it out, you will finally see it for yourself. I want to see how well you will play the role your heart lusts for. As a matter of fact, I will do this for you all. I'll make an intercession upon your behalf. Let the games begin. Play well and good luck. You will need it and more.

Tevin C. R. Dubé

In a dark day, one crack of sunlight can embody the the bliss of a heavenly divine feeling. That crack of sunshine might just happen to be a smile or one good word of encouragement.

A Silent Truth

My thoughts are always focused upon the things I would love to do for others. I guess that is the problem, I'm too selfless. Always catering to the needs of others and leaving myself undone. It's time to truly focus on me. It's time to look out for me more than ever. Therefore, I have no choice but to be selfless.

Tevin C. R. Dubé

To a careful observer, if you ever see me in love to pinpoint it out to me personally and explain the logistics of it. I am saying this because the intuitive part of me don't know what it looks, feels, smells, hears or tastes like.

A forewarning is an act of benevolence as it represents guidance. Pay close attention to yourself when you realize someone has removed that form of guidance away from you. When Nature stops its forewarning; you can soon find yourself within the eye of a storm or sudden destruction.

Tevin C. R. Dubé

The first time I went to dig yam; it was a whole new world. The digging was relentless; if the yam breaks you can feel the pain in your heart. The danger was real after I walked upon a monster mapepire snake, then at another time, a ten-footer snake. After that entire ordeal, the weight to be carried and distance is another daunting factor. But the greatest tasks are dealing with the freeloaders and price breakers who never take into consideration all of the above. I choose to give it away for free just to avoid a anger many would never truly understand.

ny story that is being told to you without any solid evidence or your immediate presence is to be utilized as a concept to be applied rather than to be established as a thesis for a blind form of believable ignorance. The story could be real and still be very far from the truth.

Tevin C. R. Dubé

You want to know when you are becoming in tune with Nature? When a common fowl has her baby chicks and you alone can pass every time without her motherly instinct identifying you as a threat to be given the pecking of a lifetime. Wild creatures starts approaching you because they no longer sense you as a threat.

A Silent Truth

When I was younger I looked at a soursop fruit and wondered why it was called such. After one fell from the tree, my curiosity peaked and I finally decided to see what made sour the soursop. To my surprise it was far sweeter beyond my expectations. It superseded its own title and I was a bit confused as to who decided to give it such a contradicting name. Then I understood. People would judge your exterior without even giving themselves the opportunity to witness firsthand the sweetness that lies deep within a soul hidden.

Tevin C. R. Dubé

The beauty of a root is overlooked by the appealing flowers atop. The lesson that exists is that a hidden beauty would always be long-lasting because only those with eyes to see shall truly treasure such a picturesque rarely beheld.

A Silent Truth

Many ask me which one of my books are the greatest. I smile outwardly but with a great deal of merriment within. The greatest out of all my books is the man standing behind it all.

Tevin C. R. Dubé

I was born from a natural royalty and the temporal ruling powers of the world suppressed it. I know that I was born a King but they stole my crown of gold. So I allowed my royalty by nature to fixate and construct it by hair. They still tried to suppress it. I knew that I was divine in flesh and they tried to suppress it. So I allowed the natural royalty within me to be my guidance and it made me to move mountains. The problem that remains is that a natural royalty cannot be suppressed forever because it is a force left untamed even though it choose to channel Itself into a temporal form of physical matter; a finite apparatus of flesh that is yet still infinite within itself.

Even though I have an average foot size of about eight and a half, many are still unable to walk within my shoes even though their feet may fit comfortably.

Tevin C. R. Dubé

Listen carefully to when you speak. You cannot want someone to adhere to you when you can't even listen to your own self.

A Silent Truth

If you cannot
identify silently the
different vibes
given off in a
room, then it
means that you
are not fully
in sync with
yourself.

After mustering up the strength, I was ready to confess to a girl how I felt as we spoke one night.

Me: "Place your hand by your heart."

Her: Chuckling at the strange gesture she asked, "Why?"

Me: "Please…..could you do it?"

Her: "Okay!"

Me: "Do you feel your heart beating?"

Her: "Yes, I feeling it."

Me: "Well that's me knocking waiting for you to let me in."

A Silent Truth

Two lines to help you get by when others has forsaken you:
1) You can never own something that has never belonged to you.
2) How could you lose something when you by yourself have never found it in the first place to begin with.

Those that are for you will find every possible reason within their ability to be at your side during all times.

Tevin C. R. Dubé

A few years ago I was craving for the taste of a watermelon over a few weeks. As the watermelon van travelled through our area I was anxious to get my hands upon it. The money I had was sufficient enough to only get half of one that was average. What pained me the most that day was that there were so many children around with hope in their eyes and not all would be able to receive. It was difficult for me not being able to give any because I didn't want some thinking that I was favouring amongst them. I know it breeds envy and jealousy but it taught me a great lesson in more ways than one. Life sometimes separates us to allow us to inherit and enjoy the things we truly deserve because the purest decisions can be the most difficult ones to make.

The greatest trap in this peculiar planet called Earth is attachment.

Tevin C. R. Dubé

When I was completing my third book, my fairly new laptop began to malfunction. It glitch, numbers kept automatically appearing, keys were no longer responding to my fingers. I became frustrated when I was locked out from own computer. But then I quieted the mind…..amidst the entire calamity, I managed to pull off my best work yet. Having stilled my mind I became the eye of the storm. Even though today not a single key works I never allowed that to dismay and sway me away from my duty. I was a born miracle that was designed to make miracles come through. Sometimes even we can forget to remember the importance of who we truly are.

No man has ever won the battle with Ego. But the one person Ego respects is a man that is filled with pure humility. Ego is eternally humbled by the presence of it.

Tevin C. R. Dubé

From the moment you and someone are having a discussion and they utter the phrase "You must always win" when common sense is prevailing, distant your tongue at once. That person is a threat to your wellbeing because they know not the true meaning of the word 'reasoning.' Such a mindset is someone who always wants to win because they are in silent competition.

A Silent Truth

There comes a time in everyone's life when their night turns to day. As this mysterious light gives a sight beyond sight to uncover the conceited and hidden agendas against you it is not with the intent that your heart should be troubled. It is a gift that is being given to signify that you are on the verge of a major breakthrough. It is the final exam to be written but only through the compassions of humility you may truly succeed by being still within your soul. If it is being unveiled before your eyes be joyful in your weakness because it entails that the solution too is forthcoming naturally.

Tevin C. R. Dubé

In a DVD club I had a conversation with a pundit's son who had converted to Christianity. And he was talking about good and evil.

I took up a movie and I drew a scenario to him. I asked, "If I find this movie to be totally good and you find this movie to be totally bad, what have we created?" I answered, "War!" I proceeded, "What is the fine line that rests between what is considered to be good and what is considered to be evil?" I answered, "Balance! Therefore, if we both reason with one another by keeping an open ear, we both may understand each other's point of view and concept. What have we created?" I answered, "Peace! There is no good and no evil. There is a state of being balanced and imbalanced.

A Silent Truth

It is an evolutionary
process that
represents both the
opportunity for further
growth spiritually and
physically. You can
call this natural mystic
by its rightful name,
Experience; but
to the many, The Spirit
of Revelation.

Tevin C. R. Dubé

The metamorphosis of a butterfly is so unique. As it emerges from the cocoon, it is stuck because it needs to push on through so that the fluids could be drained out as it struggles and squeezes its way out. If anyone interrupts that process, the butterfly would be unable to fly. Moral of the story is, sometimes our struggles are things within us that holds back our true potential. Fear, hate, envy, jealousy, malice, and pride are heavy to the soul that was designed for flight. Guess what, no one can cleanse you of such impurities save it be that of you.

A Silent Truth

Don't always look forward for the help of others, disappointments could make you bitter. Just remember they could be the reason you never succeed. And don't always want to help every single person you perceive to be in need. When your spirit feels free, it is at that moment you take heed. Critical thinking is such a beautiful gift because it is a Universal key.

Tevin C. R. Dubé

When I was searching for God I began looking all over. My hunt led me on a wild goose chase. I learned many things as I looked for God in the trees and throughout the Earth and into space and then into other galaxies. And while I was on this wild goose chase, God was being amused at my endeavours silently and I so foolishly never understood. I was searching everywhere and forgot the most important place. I learned many great things but it was until I looked within myself, then and there I found the greatest things. God had been with me looking for God the whole time. God was hidden right behind my eyelid laughing as we were both searching for ourselves together; the wild goose.

A Silent Truth

Sometimes the power we are so desperately in search of blinds us to not even realize that we had already possessed it.

As I was on my way to work one day, I saw a beetle struggling on its back alongside the road. I flipped it over because I knew it would eventually die. Another day I saw a lizard got trapped in a barrel of water, as it panicked, I placed my hands and saved it because I knew eventually it would have died. We have the power to save many lives and sometimes we are too blinded to see.

Don't be worried by those who walk around proudly thinking that they are better than others. There is no limit to the height you could attain in Life. Anyone could aspire to reach the brass ring but not too many have mastered the art of limbo.

Tevin C. R. Dubé

My cousin was given a job to do some mortar work on a man's house. So I was given a few days' work. The man had built his home in a once forested area on family land in which he had inherited after removing trees and levelling the land. As we worked one day, he became aggravated by the ants marching through the newly built house. Using some choice words he expressed himself saying, "These ants is real pest. I will kill them out." I asked, "Why you just want to kill them out?" "Because they bothering me. And I don't care. It have all the rest of land and place to go but they find nowhere else but to pass through my house. I want to move in my house in a while and watch them now." I calmly responded, "Them have life too, so we does can't think so. Sometimes we does have to see things differently." "How you mean different?" he said irately, "They could pass somewhere else, you not making any sense to me right now." "Okay." I initially said. "But remember

A Silent Truth

it is you who choose to come where
they were living first, destroy their
home to build yours because you thought
that your family is more important than
them because we are humans and them
is just ants. But they are entitled to the
Earth just as much as you and me but
we don't see it like that because we are
full of ego. How you would feel after
you finish your house and something
comes and remove you and your
family from it without any care if you
live or die because it considers itself
superior to us because we are considered
to be just humans to them. Take a good
look, the ants just passing through
your house now because they are
looking for a new home. Follow the line
and you would see they not living in your
house, they are just passing through."
He then said calmly, "Boy, you really different
because I never woulda see it the
way how you see it and say it like that."

Tevin C. R. Dubé

The greatest battle you will ever face is the confrontation of your own self. As you mirror yourself, every move is already anticipated. Your actions are already being reflected. Going head to head your defeat is inevitable. Sometimes, the greatest battles won are as a result of an embrace. Acceptance!

A Silent Truth

A balanced being is as a result of a mastered subconscious. A mastered subconscious is as a result of effectively communicating with your intuition. Paying perfect attention to the purity of your intuition is as a result of becoming in tune with your Higher Self. Becoming in tune with your Higher Self is as a result of becoming aligned with Nature. To become aligned with Nature is as a result of becoming One with the entire Universe. Becoming One with the entire Universe is as a result of being directly absorbed into The Great Beyond. Being a part of The Great Beyond is as a result of being reduced into Nothing. Becoming Nothing is as a result of being Humble. And to be Humble is to become the very source of All Existence. The source of All Existence is as a result of infinity within infinity infinitely.

Tevin C. R. Dubé

What actually is the true art of time travel? Today you are the future self to that in which you were yesterday. Remember when the person yesterday was so eager to be the future you today? Remember the dreams you had yesterday are the reality of today? Remember the double mind that was pleading with you not to make that move yesterday because it would be affecting you today? Yes! Time travel is when the future is responding to the calls of the past. But they are both a creation of today.

A Silent Truth

Today you can now understand that voice that was warning you not to make that move because it is humbugging you today. Today you are grateful that you followed your intuition because you are being benefitted today. Today you can now talk life back into the old you which simultaneously is the future creation of the new you. Time travel is nothing more than the communication between that of your Higher Self and your Lower Self. When you are able to combine both, that's when you become Absolute.

Tevin C. R. Dubé

I was being pushed to the precipice and was made to take one step further. As I plummeted towards rock bottom, I indeed panicked within my soul. But during mid-fall, I quieted my heavens; all my life I made myself to walk so I had to be reminded that I still had wings to fly.

A Silent Truth

There is a pause between each second. What is that pause to be exact? That pause is a timeless state in which time itself emulates from one second unto another. How can I access this timeless state as a mere mortal instrument of flesh? The answer is simple, through the process of Critical Thinking.

The most powerful force that was given unto man is the Power of Mind. Such a power can solely be activated by imagination. The Power of Mind is the ability to 'Will' things into Existence. It is the direct access to the Spiritual Mechanisms to which is the fundamental stages of any given blueprint. In other words, the Power of Mind is the ability to Create Any and Every and All Things.

A Silent Truth

How fictional is the flash? Or should I ask how fictional are you? An atom is consisted of a bunch of subatomic particles. We are consisted of a bunch of subatomic particles that form atoms, which form cells, which form blood, tissues and organs in which we have an entire unit called the body. All was initially matter in the form of gases. To get a solid is as a result of atoms vibrating at different frequencies. Therefore, if one could gain full control of every atom in which they are made up of, even the flash will pale in comparison to the accomplishment of what I may call a Superhuman Supreme Being.

Tevin C. R. Dubé

The Earth is a mere trinket to the entire Universe. Fighting over the Earth for sovereignty is like owning an entire gold chain and yet still you are trying to prove a point by focusing your attention upon a specific link and claiming that to be yours. How foolish the minds of mere mortals work?

A Silent Truth

Sometimes some things are just unexplainable. The only way you can truly understand it is to experience it directly. Like for instance, if I were to ask what is a colour? One may explain it through visual demonstration. But if I were to ask, by let's say, could you explain what the colour blue is? I'm for certain to never be answered because an answer could never be given for something that doesn't truly exist. So in keeping that in mind, have you ever wondered what a newborn baby is smiling about? Well if you do, so too am I. Don't expect me to have the answers to everything.

Tevin C. R. Dubé

Miracles can and do only exist under one condition; to those who truly believe and work towards the expectancy for it to take place. Then and there the true magic of miracles often takes place.

How can you identify someone as naïve? If someone eats and drinks anything, is lazy, get sick and then pray to God for a long life, health and strength. But continues the same trend and still expects a miraculous touch. A fool is best identified by their inability to utilize a natural gift called common sense.

Tevin C. R. Dubé

Just thinking about an old notion inherited from generation to generation. 'Don't eat out from a pot because it will have lots of rain on your wedding day.' Well I guess I'll have to build an ark to get married in. Noah is already one of my nicknames.

Life is a

continuous toil

and Death is

the enjoyment

of it all.

Life is a repeat of events to be mastered in many different forms and fashions.

A Silent Truth

The blessing that most
human beings at first
see as a curse is the
the fact that one day we all
have to die. The only
way to be a human is
that you must be given
birth to. That is the one
and only natural way but
to truly become any
and everything, Death is the
only possibility.
Why do you think
there are so many
exits but one
main entrance?

Tevin C. R. Dubé

A a man might look at
a heap of pebbles
and just see stones.
Another may look at
it and just see a heap of
gravel. Another
might look at it and
see the potential for
a house. It is such a
blessing to always
be open-minded.

Life is a meditation of the Spirit in general. The maintenance of the body is as a result of an involuntarily yet still a consciously meditative state of the Spirit—that is the master of all things that are still subjected unto being mastered itself by itself.

Tevin C. R. Dubé

Long ago, I wanted to develop my patience so I started fishing. I learned that it was all a mindset. After that discovery I began to master my thoughts by first acknowledging all the things that seem to get the best of me by taking away all its power. It was the art of peaceful confrontation in mind by paying them no mind.

A Silent Truth

The system would gladly support a comedian because they could create a jester out of them. It would gladly support an actor because it could create many different characters out of them. It would gladly support a mainstream entertainer because it could create idols out of them. It would gladly support politicians because it could create a mockery out of nations. With all this in mind, there is nothing comedic neither scripted nor entertaining and political about being awake. This, the system could never gladly support. The truth must either be perfectly tucked behind jokes, hidden in between scripted lines or be watered down by elaborate speeches. In no way must it ever be plain for all to see. The system only needs a few alive to maintain a sleeping death amongst the many.

Tevin C. R. Dubé

One day an old man breathing
never in his life had paid
attention to the fact that
breathing was such a precious
thing. It wasn't until he was
passing away, in his last
moments as he was gasping for
air, he realized how much he had
never appreciated the simple
the fact that he could breathe. How
many times many of us
wait until something or someone
is finally gone for good until we
realize that showing appreciation
is something great to be perfected
through the practice of showing
it daily until it mainly becomes
involuntarily as breathing.

A Silent Truth

Let it is made clear to the world that any man who finds fault with another without cause to examine his own being because he may well be at fault with himself.

Tevin C. R. Dubé

I guess your attitude truly determines your altitude. I treated my school bag with reverence because I knew my education was the only thing I had to alleviate my situation. I never placed it on the ground; I never sat on it or my books and I never placed my feet upon it. I never allowed myself such a luxury so that could explain my attitude towards anyone who stepped out of line. A few years later I graduated as the top student of my high school. When I sacrificed and bought new clothes, I wore them only on special occasions because I knew how hard it was for me to acquire them. As a result of such, years passed and my clothes and shoes looked new brand but I looked different every time in the eyes of others. As I received my notepad as a gift at my graduation, I inherited the inspiration to write because I was so determined to understand my purpose.

It was the least but I hallowed it.

A little over five years I became a published author. If someone asks me, "Are you going down the road?" my response is, "I'm not going down. I'm going in the shop, I don't go down."

"Are you going up the road?" "Yes, that is the only direction I'm going. Up." When I wash my clothes, I hang it up facing forward and in an upright manner ensuring that it is not left inside out. I don't ever use the word poor to describe myself growing up; I said we just don't have it right now. When I gave up, was when I needed rest but I never yet quit in my thoughts.

Tevin C. R. Dubé

Don't always be willing to appreciate me as soon as I am about to leave or after I have gone. What about the times when I was there.

A Silent Truth

When things seem to be hopeless, I would utter don't worry, something great will happen. Now this never meant that I never had doubts, fears, and regrets or have been pessimistic and been plagued with over-thinking. Detrimental situations are like tinder and sometimes a little optimism can become the spark to burn it all away. Your attitude truly determines your altitude but your actions about the simplest things do establish and build your character as a human being.

Tevin C. R. Dubé

When the spirit talks it's amazing for I was in my beginning years at my high school when the late former Prime Minister Patrick Manning came to visit. I was excited to finally see the man, who had truly been a father to the fatherless. I was honoured to see him for all the things he did for me as a fatherless child. As he walked up to the main entrance of the school, I stood along the wayside as many other students swarmed to lay their hands upon him. His bodyguards were commanding and debarring students from touching him as they tried to curb the buzzing crowd. He spoke sternly but in a cool manner, "Leave them. They are children and they are happy to see their Prime Minister. What is the worst they could do to

A Silent Truth

me? Stab me with a pen!"
As I took control of my actions, I could
not react as the other students
even though I may have been more excited
than all. So I stood on the side of the
main entrance away as he proceeded
upwards to where I stood. Both our eyes
met four and he seemed to be intrigued by the
sight of me. I was calm on the surface
but the admiration I had was great towards
him because I saw his vision and I was
a part of it. My self-esteem was
so low it was a shame but I kept my head
erect. He left the entire crowd and came
over to me who chose to stand away
from all. "Why are you not trying to touch
me like the other students?" he asked
with calm anticipation as he extended
his hand towards me. I answered my hero
as we shook hands, "Because you are a man
just like everybody else." In astonishment,
he exclaimed, "You hear what this young
man said to me?" His entourage was

bedazzled because they were unaware. As he held my hands firmly he moved in closer, "You are the most intelligent person I met thus far and I met a lot of great people all over the world. You are by far the most intelligent student in this entire school and I would not be surprised to hear that one day you top this school." He never even knew that years before this meeting, he had offered my mother a ride as she was awaiting a taxi along the Marabella route to attend YTEPP classes when my brothers and I were much younger. He was only a Minister at the time and my mother spoke highly about his kindness. Years later, his prophecy to me was indeed, fulfilled even though I was at first rejected from that same school. Indeed, I graduated atop of the school academics. As his health deteriorated over the years, I wanted to recollect this entire ordeal with him. About 9 months before his passing,

A Silent Truth

I had a dream. We both had a long
conversation with Harris Promenade,
San Fernando to Indian Walk.
I told him all I had to say to him and we
had a lengthy spiritual conversation. But
as soon as we reached Paynter Cemetery,
he spoke his last before disappearing. As I
awoke, I told my mother that he was prepping
to leave this Life and now more than ever
I wanted to meet with him in person again.
Even though I loathe politics I was now
an O.J.T. in a constituency office. I guess he
was spiritually grooming me for it because
I could never recall all the things he had
said to me. It was now a couple of months
since I commenced my duties there.
I had chosen an auspicious day to keep my
first book launch, on the morning of
on July 2nd, 2016 he passed away and I
would host my first-ever
book launch event.

Tevin C. R. Dubé

There comes a time when Noah's the ark must be completely shut. No longer must you give permission to ungrateful people to enter into your life. You cannot be the only person ensuring that other people's dreams come through at the expense of yours being delayed or completely stopped. Sometimes you must allow your heart to be consumed by Medusa petrifying gaze. If both you and your neighbours' homes are leaking and you have a block to solve yours, is it a good thing to take pity on their request and leave yours undone? There is a great difference between being truly humble and absolutely stupid. There is a great difference between stooping low to conquer and lying down to be conquered.

A Silent Truth

I have the appearance of the moon. I may appear to be dull at times but can suddenly be illuminated as a full moon. My anger can be crimson red as a blood moon or I can become like the dark side of it. At times I can be Super and the next I'm eclipsed. I can magnify the light of others as well as snuff it out completely. The tides listen to me. All I am saying is that I have experienced the fullness of every emotion within me but just like the moon, my energy can be felt but I choose to be stationary with a strong sense of electromagnetism.

I sold my gold

to achieve

my goal.

A Silent Truth

Sometimes I do tell myself, it was battles you were facing but after escaping from the valley to be upon a mountaintop retreat; all I could see was that it was an all-out war all along.

Tevin C. R. Dubé

When the man who is always strong for everyone gets weak, his weakness is a very different type of weakness. Sometimes the saviour is in dire need of a saviour as well. Sometimes, our heroes need a good word of encouragement without any request. Even a strong man needs to be cuddled and hugged. Sometimes all they need is your ears and less of your tongue. An open ear produces words of impeccable timing, such as, 'I understand' can be a mountain of gold.

A Silent Truth

Dangling by a thread! This tiny line is a life force that can still hold the entire weight of a behemoth. Sometimes in Life, this thin thread can be strengthened by someone giving hope to another. Sometimes it is a little smile or a kind word or an open ear. You may never know who is dangling by their last thread.

As people exit your life, don't see it as if they had forsaken you even though such may be the case. They are actually creating space for the right ones to enter.

Space is a necessary component for the process of creation to take place. Many of us are unable to achieve our fullest potential because our lives are too clustered. A cumbersome mind is like a confusion of natural elements.

Tevin C. R. Dubé

As we intake Life's breath or what we commonly referred to as oxygen, as we do absorb it, in return, we exhale Death in the form of carbon dioxide. I see myself as a tree because as I intake the waste product of others, I am able to reproduce a breath of fresh air. People don't truly appreciate the the extent to those who dump their burdens upon or to those who they always run too for strength in their times of need. They are the ones who have to intake your burdens just as a tree do with our carbon dioxide as they create comfort or a solution. They have to work hard internally like a tree but in a mental sense. But remember trees too need oxygen as they would sacrifice their day to only recuperate in the night

A Silent Truth

by taking in less than the amount that was given. They give you more than they could ever possibly receive. Most times many cut down, slash and burn, disrespect and forsake them. But in the end their lifespan is being cut shorter and shorter while the trees mysteriously lives on eternally.

Tevin C. R. Dubé

When the Earth is in distress and it cries out for help, Nature presents natural stabilisers that we call natural disasters. So in keeping that in mind, being in the the natural order of things, when I'm in distress and I cry out, too begin to see natural wonders occurring in my favour as well.

 t times you want die, then at other intervals you want to live. This confusion creates right the occurrence for untimely occurrences.

Tevin C. R. Dubé

Sometimes I feel like the Spirit and I are too attached. I sometimes feel like it deliberately makes me feel lonely so that I have no choice but to seek counsel from It. At times I feel as if it becomes jealous of the the fact that if I finally inherit the things I so longed for; it cannot have me all to Itself. So, at times I see the end of the road to human existence and the more I see the more I realize that this life makes no sense to truly be a part of. But the more I remain in flesh, my heart still desires to live a normal human life because of the many potential involved. Sometimes the Spirit feels like departing but the soul doesn't want to be caught up in the veil of regrets pondering upon what if. This mind is confusing. I now see the importance of the two words taken lightly, "Be Still." We must truly never be anxious for nothing and allow the process to naturally take its course.

The one word that is multilingual and Universal is the the word 'No'. Yet still many cannot interpret and understand it. Many are unaware of how to efficiently use it and when to effectively say it.

Tevin C. R. Dubé

The reasons why I'm a big supporter of Drake because his realest songs resonate with me. What he is experiencing is the same things that I'm facing right now. Songs like 'Fake Love' and 'God's Plan' are facts and a testament to the things a honest and trying man has to face from malicious, envious and jealous people who only pray for you to fail and look forward to your downfall. It was God's Plan to cripple the wicked pharaoh off his seat. It was God's Plan who caused Saul to be dethroned by his own hands.

There are already 7 deadly sins and some people choose to make themselves altogether eight.

Some of us will surely die, some of us shall be reborn, and some of us shall go on to exist forevermore. The decision is all yours to make.

A Silent Truth

The Spirit has borne witness to the treacherous nature of the flesh for tens of millions of years and more. That's why it is fearless as to the offences of man because it already has infinite solutions to solve anything that confronts the man of spirit or to better yet be paraphrased, the spirit man or the spirited being experiencing human existence. Each vessel is a new under the face of the sun but the Spirit is ever of old. Just as politicians are pawns to a system of old proportions. Until your eyes are truly opened: Puppets; either to nature or to slavery. One is natural and the other is manmade.

Tevin C. R. Dubé

There are two types of slaves. There are those who are enslaved to nature because they are scared to take control of their destiny. These are ones who never truly know themselves. Then there are those enslaved to the system. The biggest slaves are the politicians who lack true vision, creativity, innovation and good governance not of an economy but that of themselves. They may trick the general public with many fallacies but at the expense of their own souls becoming imprisoned by ego, pure lust, lies, hypocrisy, and insatiable greed. Thank God Patrick Manning did it with grace because he understood balance in Life. Eat little, clear your path while ensuring that the majority are satisfied in the process.

A Silent Truth

Those of old always stated that one thing your house must never run short of salt. From that moment on, I say that your mind must never run short of ideas, thoughts of creativity and ingenuity as much as your house must never be lacking pens and blank paper to be stained with written ink.

Tevin C. R. Dubé

International, already I Am. Worldwide, already I Am. Legendary, already I Am. Successful, already I Am. Everything I want to become and more already I Am. All my dreams and aspirations, already I Am. Regardless of my position at the moment in Life, already I Am That I Am. Sometimes all you have to do is just put it out into the Universe with a strong sense of belief and a hard-working wave of energy. Then look and see, already I Am That I Am.

A Silent Truth

We live in a world where we first endanger an entire species and after it has become extinct, we find self-righteous reasons to justify our actions.

Tevin C. R. Dubé

It is truly amazing when you have just about given up on everything except for leaving yourself to be mysteriously used for whatever purposes that may truly be beneficial unto others and no longer only yourself. That is the true commencing of your spiritual experiences that is to be had within a human vessel.

A Silent Truth

The number one killer and destroyer of man is as a result of emotions. Some are a little too sensitive whilst others lack compassion. As too much of one thing isn't good for nothing, in the same exactitude too little is a danger. Things of all sorts happen not for the bitterness of a soul to have a bombarded spirit. If you know you are a divine being, then one shall see it as only a gathering of data to be transported spiritually.

Tevin C. R. Dubé

There is no
need for a
solution when
you are already
the answer
you've been
searching for.

Imagine a world without a Bible, or Quran, or Bhagavad Gita. There was once a time when the entire world was just in peace—just enlightened beings enjoying pure spirituality.

Tevin C. R. Dubé

What's for me will always be for me. If I'm halfway across the heart, it will find me. If it is truly meant for me, I might even stumble upon it by human accident but still through a pure alignment. Regardless of how it happens, what's for me will always be for me. There is no such thing as coincidence to a perfectly aligned Universe.

A Silent Truth

There is an infinite world, with infinite possibilities, with infinite happenings in between the unaccounted time betwixt the intervals from one second to the other.

Tevin C. R. Dubé

We shall see our way and when we begin to see our way, we would be out of people's way. And if people try to get in our way, they shall be mysteriously removed from the way. That is the way of the way itself.

A Silent Truth

Being humble is knowing exactly when to walk away, remain quiet, portraying excellent endurance through long suffering, always demonstrating forgiveness, executing critical thinking, listens well and is slow to speak, swift in thoughts and slow towards mindless actions. But don't ever mix up humility with stupidity. A man could never enter into your home and tell you to leave and that your time is up or takes your vehicle and says that you have to walk from now on as you continue to watch him drive boldly. No! Even the humblest man will not watch such a thing take place with him and humbly walk away and then turn around to deem their act of utter stupidity to that of humility.

Tevin C. R. Dubé

It is such a beautiful sight when your eyes are open and you can see everything. It's such a beautiful sight when you can always decipher the good from the bad and the bad from the ugly. O the magnificence of sight beyond sight.

A Silent Truth

Some people hide their faces behind flowers, others behind money, some behind vanity, others behind a mask, some behind makeup. The thing is you can easily hide your face but your true colours, the hidden ones emulate with such a great force, not even the ones hiding behind their disguises can truly keep it concealed for too long. The truth is both a revealing light to the dark as much as it is the darkness to a confounding light source.

Tevin C. R. Dubé

Imagine I watching Woody Woodpecker when Mother Nature had demoted him to a pigeon after he was not fulfilling his natural duties. The trainer pigeon said to him in his quest to be promoted back into a woodpecker, "I knew you were a sucker from the word wood." The things fed to our subconscious mind early on do have a great impact on us in our adult stage. A sleeping sheep stays in the comforts of a barn but to be quickly stripped naked and be easily led to a slaughterhouse.

A Silent Truth

To always be led by a shepherd is to always be at the mercy of that shepherd. To the sheep that is brave enough to venture into the wilderness at the mercy of ravenous beasts, none is more ferocious, wild and untamed as the silent forces of Nature.

Tevin C. R. Dubé

Attending to funerals in the past, I dressed for the occasion but now as I attend, I dress to impress. "Like you going to raise the dead?" is an infamous question that is usually asked. And my response was, "Yes I Am." I dress as if it is truly a celebration because to me, only a sleeping soul and a dead mind is afraid to explore the beauty in the things that are shrouded by mysteries. A hidden beauty once found is an image that could never be forgotten. It is like the hidden anatomy of a naked the body once revealed to the eyes, it could never be unseen. Consider Death as the spiritual medulla oblongata.

A Silent Truth

At first I was mortified at the sight of a soul without motion lying in a wooden box. The thought to think that one day I too shall be within one are enough to scare the daylight out of the sun within my soul because of the blackened fears of my carnal mind. Upon the realization that death is a choice, I no longer see a motionless victim but I see a loud victor shouting in silence as a gentle breeze. Those who passed away are true heroes because they conquered the ultimate fear. Death! They are no longer afraid because it is they who have chosen to yield up the ghost and now the fearful are left behind to mourn someone who has already won the ultimate war whilst they continue to fight a frivolous battle with fear by longing to be forever in the wretched form of flesh. "Let the dead bury the dead."

Tevin C. R. Dubé

The greatest part of Nature is the pure consciousness of Nature itself. If you want to be circumcised from it is to simply live an unconscious and unnatural life. Pure consciousness is not just the key foundation to Life but it is the very master key which unlocks the infinite gateway to All perpetuating Existences eternally.

A Silent Truth

My mother is my greatest inspiration. Everything which I've accomplished thus far was and is still because of her. I was a very observant child and acknowledged my parent's struggles long before my father came and passed away while I was at the tender age of 9. One day, as I saw my mother struggle to stitch my sneakers for school, she couldn't have held it in as she broke down in tears right before my eyes. I hugged and said to her, "Ma, don't cry. Everything is going to be alright." I was in form 3 and from that day, my passion grew ten times stronger to help her. I persevered and gained 6 out of my 8 CXC subjects at first. I worked, resend myself to school, and after 2 years, I graduated atop the academics back in high school in CAPE Advanced Studies. Every time, I received an accolade,

Tevin C. R. Dubé

as soon as I left the stage, I proceeded over to my mother's seat before all in attendance and gave it to her saying, "Ma, this is yours." It was my subliminal message to her that all this is because of you. It was hers to keep for all her hard work and sacrifice. She wanted me to but I allowed her to hold onto all the things I'd received it because I wanted her to feel proud. I left with my hands free even though all the other students wanted to make a statement holding onto theirs for many others to see. But the impact I left on all after my valedictory speech and my selfless actions was my deep sense of humility. Today, I have a combined amount of 16 passes. As I continued to endure painstakingly because of her in which my efforts in finding myself led me to become a naturally professional writer. My tutor became my intuition and now this shepherd boy David slew another

A Silent Truth

mammoth, Goliath. After more than 5 years, I officially published my first book. In the year 2017, I was now collecting a First Time Author Award which the Prime Minister of our country would also be collecting one as well. On that day, I was on a level playing field with the leader of our nation. The only difference was he wrote his first book as a well-established man but I fully established myself as a nobody. But upon receiving that award, I gave it to my mother also, it was to serve as a reminder that I'm still working on permanently alleviating her struggles. I haven't gotten to that point just yet but guess what, this little shepherd boy is leading himself through the wilderness and will establish his oasis in which many deserted shall drink.

Tevin C. R. Dubé

It was God's Plan to make Pharaoh loses his entire kingdom. It was God's Plan that made Saul dethrone himself. They both lost it because of their own self-righteous actions. The first fought against a man of the Spirit and the latter were jealous of a little shepherd boy who was chosen by the spirit who in return came out from nowhere to slaughter Goliath. The concept behind those stories can be applied in today's society. The high and mighty are not only those in power but most times it resides in those who are low and humble. It took David around 15 years before he became King but went on to rule for 4 decades after that 15 years, Saul was no longer a ruler forever.

A Silent Truth

There are those who are persistent like flies and gnats. Some claim to be the alpha male whilst others proclaim to be at the top of the food chain. Once you reside beneath Nature under the order of physicality, you are always subjected to the inevitability of change and hence you are very much a part of the food chain itself.

Tevin C. R. Dubé

Let us say that you were meant to live forever, to be immortalized in the flesh as is. Then what? Let's say 1,000 years have passed. By then you would have experienced the pleasures of sex in its entirety. You would surely become more than wealthy because amassing it would be less of a challenge because you are no longer a pupil being mandated by time. You would have learnt a substantial amount of knowledge concerning many great things. Then what? Let us say that 10,000 years have passed by, you would experience it all and everything would surely become a bore. You would have been a God to many but would surely experience the ways of a Devil. You would have come to witness the constant cycle of birth and decay. All of the people you knew are long gone. You would outlive

every single one of your children and
their generations eternally. You would
no longer have the pleasure to be a
human. You would become more than
a prisoner within a freedom many
would so foolishly love to attain
thinking that immortality of the flesh
is beautiful but if it is attained, how long
shall it be loved? Once a blessing but
now a curse; what you would surely
realise is the fact that to be a human is
to not even make it past the shores of
discoveries unto an ocean of limitless
possibilities. Nature is so abundantly
exceeding with Love to never make
one man to be a slave to it but to be
given the chance to become a
free and untamed force by becoming
One with it. But through such
immortality, you would soon realise
that the flesh is already immortalised
through continuous birth but as for the
life force we all share is altogether the

same source. Nowhere is still Somewhere and Nothing is still Something. To not be is still to be. To not do is still to do. No man has ever seen the wind but that doesn't deter him from breathing it. The air could be the vilest looking thing but we breathe it bravely without prejudice. We fear Death through misconceptions. New beginnings come through the retiring of old things, to be immortalized in the flesh is far much greater a punishment. It is like continuously living through suicide but without death as the ultimate escape. Hence see why there is only one way to truly be a human but multiple ways that lead to infinity. Human existence is finitely-infinite but Death is the gateway that leads unto an existence that is infinitely-infinite.

A Silent Truth

Is it a weird thing that I had a dream or more of a profound vision while my body was at rest during sleep when I saw myself teaching Prophet Mohammed, The Buddha and the ancient Chinese philosopher by the name Lao Tzu. If not, well best believe I was teaching each of them before their respective journeys had begun. They were my pupils at one point in a past existence.

Tevin C. R. Dubé

Some years ago I learnt an important lesson early one morning. Being a very well-organised person, my operations are time efficient. I had some important errands to run, so as usual, I put everything in place the night before. Early the next morning, I got ready and was about to leave home at the agreed time I initially set in my mind. Eerily so, as soon as I was about to leave, I felt I was forgetting something.

I double and triple-checked and everything was there. As I proceeded towards the door, a temporal form of insanity struck me and I was pacing to and fro in my home in a confounded manner. No matter what I did, it was like I was being debarred from leaving. When I came too, I sat down, calmed my profound confusion, and turned on the television. It was already on MTV2 music channel and I thought to myself,

Tevin you need to relax, it's not the right time to leave home as yet. Rap Attack was on and some of my favourite hip-hop acts were on at the same time. After 5 minutes of hiatus, I felt that eerie and oddly confusing feeling depart from me. I was now comfortable within my spirit to leave. As soon as I arrived at the junction to get a taxi, there was a little commotion. I asked one of the gas station attendants what just happened. He said, "If you were here less than five minutes ago, yuh woulda see ah accident. De man crash sudden dey, it happen so fast eh." Exactly where the car struck, is exactly where commuters stand awaiting transportation. Indeed, if I had left home that 5 minutes earlier, I would have been in time to be a part of that accident. With that sudden impact at such a close range distance from the main road, I would have been caught off-guard, pinned between the car and the concrete barrier to maintain traffic flow into the gas station. That day I'd learnt so many valuable lessons. Sometimes a little setback is an even greater blessing as much as being a little spontaneous and never too organized always sticking to the script. Life is all about balance.

Every man has his own destruction to face. Be not troubled if others are putting you through the test first. Once you have endured the process, it is you who would be given the front row tickets to witness theirs. It is your choice to sit back and look on or be compassionate to help another to make it through. The Natural Mystic called Life.

Tevin C. R. Dubé

My God Chi is fully awakened every a single time I face any adversity and push on through. I can feel the force that is round about me. My inner Divine has become fully awakened to the more I dance the dance of death while I am yet still alive. My life is testament to this fact. Up until this point, when others face off against me, they unlock hidden powers within my soul and at the expense of their ignorance, I gain more spiritual bliss. After such, I am more open and receptive to silent communications of the Great Beyond. I inherit more and more divine inspiration after I'd forged a mutable relationship with Death itself by having hands-on experience with it. It has helped me to surpass my God Chi stage unto the unlocking of

A Silent Truth

the Great Divine Spirit within me in
all Its splendour—for now, it shall forever
be awakened in me, be with me and
has become me. A living embodiment who
have attained a fusion with the very
source of Existence Itself. Son
Goku in the flesh.

Tevin C. R. Dubé

When I looked back at all the things that plagued my mind and bothered my soul, I only realised how much I've robbed myself of my own happiness. From it, I've gained more things than one. A bit of pessimism is a good thing because in Life you cannot allow your mind to become too settled, the element of surprise would always get the best of you. Secondly, I've learnt that worrying about things, before it happened is only an apparition of the mind. There is a great possibility that things can always go extremely bad but there is an even greater chance it could all work out in your favour.

A Silent Truth

Sometimes people fail to see that God's lessons can be hard lessons. Sometimes it is a lesson of Death but all the lessons of the Most High is good. Another may learn their lesson through death because of their ignorance and stubborn ways but another may learn that lesson and escape judgment because they are willing to learn and try.

nd I repeat. Leave the quiet man alone. Leave the just man alone. Leave the righteous man alone. Leave the humble man alone. The Powers of the Universe resides within such a one. The Power to create is within as well as the Power of destruction. The Great Balance can be found within him. Your destruction could very well be the Creation of something even greater.

s my inspirational juices start to rise it pours down from my cranium as a waterfall while simultaneously flowing upwards as the River Nile. Sleep becomes a nuisance to the soul because I don't like wasting precious time like that.

Tevin C. R. Dubé

My day of redemption is coming. Help or no help, that day is destined to arrive. When the hour of fight down has arrived, the throne of establishment is nigh. Open Eyesight is most blissful when the soul remains still.

If you don't have the ability to touch my soul spiritually, you don't have any right to physically touch me at all.

Tevin C. R. Dubé

You can't claim your body to be a temple without a hallowed mind. It's like a sewer line telling a the cesspool that it is only good to be filled with waste without realizing that it has to first pass through itself.

A Silent Truth

We as a people must stop look forward to another's downfall, especially if they had done you wrong. Like do attract like. If your thinking is negative towards them and they are already emitting negative frequencies into your pathway, you inevitably prevent yourself from the true blessings that lie within. Many great things you withhold from yourself.

Tevin C. R. Dubé

Do you want to know the main reason why many of us suffer and are forever oppressed? Well it'll be my pleasure to inform you of such. We always want someone to run to our rescue, we always want someone to save us. Whether it be a politician or Christ. Get up and save yourself, run to your rescue and stop depending upon others to make things happen for you. Stop creating fictitious beliefs of rescue, utilise your 'Will Power' and stop being willing to be a charity case.

A Silent Truth

How foolish the
fools think that their
heavenly apparition
has blinded me? I
see with both eyes
yes but I look
beyond with a third.
I have activated a
sight that can make
the blind to see.

Tevin C. R. Dubé

One of the greatest assets a mind could ever possess is the picture-perfect art of Imagination. In keeping that in mind, to me, an idealistic relationship is when both parties recognise the true esthetic values of each others' soul and unique individuality and learning how to perfectly blend and transition into each other just as the night into day and the day into night with none seeking autonomy—but always engages in the purity of procreation of all sorts while still learning to create and maintain perfect balance through the overstanding and adapting to each others' polarities. Every greet is met with a bow and true words of reverence between this holy couple, "Your Majesty."
"Yes, your Highness."

Even when you are behind you are still in front. It's just a matter of how your perspective works.

Tevin C. R. Dubé

If all research that

was led had find that

the first human inhabitants

of the Earth were heavily

pigmented, then who

do you think are

indigenous throughout

all the lands? The

pettiness of mankind

has superseded

the state of being retarded

by a quadruple million, billion,

trillion, zillion light years.

A Silent Truth

Receiving good prophecy through a clairvoyant manner operates something like this: it is like being placed upon a high point to find your bearings. Sometimes you maybe uncertain about good things to come into your life. Being upon this height will give you a clear overview as to where your destination resides. As you come down to continue your journey, you will come up against the thickets, valleys, mountains and ravines. But the prophesies given before your journey is to act as a stabiliser that no matter what you have to face, you will overcome because you were destined to reach your destination. The only thing is that you have to make it happen for yourself but along the way there is divine assistance to be had.

Tevin C. R. Dubé

My mind does travel so fast within the Space in my mind that sometimes it is so hard for me to return to explain the things I does be saying time and again. When you understand the nature of infinity you would soon realise that we are all speaking on the same thing but with infinite ways to express it. The summary of words may seem simple but to a deep thinker, they would be able to see an ocean of meaning behind it. I'm easily agitated when I have to explain the same thing over and over again. But at times I humble my haste to realise that many are stranded on Earth while you are exploring the vastness of space.

A Silent Truth

You can't want
to play you
more stink
than anything
when Life itself
can be a true
skunk.

Tevin C. R. Dubé

People love to say that they can't do this or be like this or live without this. Be mindful of your tongue. Your words are as a result of your tongue manipulating the air into a vibrating frequency that is transmitted into audible sounds which then transitions into syllables unto the creation of an entire word. The air is Life and your words may encourage Life to prove you wrong by taking away all the things that you so love and can't be without just approving to you that you can and should and would be able to live without anything—because many are still alive even though they are no longer a part of human existence itself.

A Silent Truth

Sometimes it is a little good to fake it till you make it. Try to keep a good look when things aren't looking good at all. Learn to keep your head up when worries are burdening you to look down. Try to keep your thoughts rich even though your situation is screaming poor. But when you make it to where you always wanted to be, remember your root days. If you are wealthy there's no need to always look good. Just always remain clean and pure in your heart. When your burdens are lifted it's time to look down in compassion. Life is all about balance.

Tevin C. R. Dubé

When you become so awakened too quickly, many times, you wish to be normal. Sometimes you wish to go back to sleep and be just like everyone else who is asleep at the crowd movements in Life. The reality is more surreal that real itself. After a man has been risen from the dead he may die again but he will surely be anything else except for being dead.

A Silent Truth

When you choose to never become conscious about Self you become a slave to Nature naturally. Ramses the Pharaoh had a lot of bad-mind towards Moses and as a result to such a low state of thinking, he couldn't even identify that he was a pawn to Nature because he wasn't even conscious of his actions. His heart was being hardened by God and he couldn't even identify that he was willingly being used to uplift an entire group of people at the expense of him willing to lose everything because he couldn't even control his bad mind. We all know how that story ended for him.

Tevin C. R. Dubé

To the man digging a pit for another, it is already being dug for himself. Remember it is him who is already within. As he creates his valley automatically you are placed upon a mountain to see him burying himself alive.

A Silent Truth

Sickness is another way of making the body to become stronger. Every time you overcome, it makes for a more formidable immune system. When you see yourself being presented with many struggles and adversities, it is nothing more than an attempt to help catapult yourself unto greatness.

Tevin C. R. Dubé

To change the world you must first learn to reconstruct an entire Universe. To reconstruct an entire Universe is through a near-perfect alignment of your thoughts. To perfectly align your thoughts, one must learn to see all things from many different perspectives as possible. Each perspective brings a whole new world of understanding. Through the establishment of a more balanced thinking, your actions are well-calculated and your words are of an immaculate and impeccable nature. As a result of changing yourself, you spark the curiosity of another's mind to be willing to change the way they think. And there you would have changed the entire world.

 cockroach is one of the very few creatures whose outer coating is radioactive resistant.

Tevin C. R. Dubé

Let us explore the common morals of life. Go to school, gain a proper education, attain a degree, get a good job, have a nice home, a vehicle to drive, get married, have kids and Life's mission has been accomplished. Then what? After you've attained such, what is the next move? To sit back and watch Life take it all away piece by piece. Life is never about the things we set out to accomplish, it is a matter of us retaining the truth about the actuality of our true selves. We are a part of the entire Universe that was created by the Universe to study the entire Universe itself. We are nothing more than envoys of data collection. Individually we were all meant to be unique analysts of the Great All in All.

A Silent Truth

There is a high probability that those who are in love with specific animals were an incarnation of such. Those who are in love with humanity are probably a reincarnated soul. Who am I to doubt anything that supersedes human interpretation and most times our misunderstandings of unexplained naturalisms? Remember all living things share the same source but not all are alive. I'm in love with Nature because I'm in love with it all. I'm in love with the purity of a consciousness infinitely perpetuating. I'm in love with an Existence that equates to Nothing that still gives way for Everything to be possible. I'm in love with Nothing just to be in love with Everything. I'm on a path leading to nowhere but to still end up any and everywhere.

Tevin C. R. Dubé

lways remember,
the higher the
flames the less
smoke is emitted.
Get rid of
everything that
stifles your fires
unto a pile of ash and
a high plume of
smoke.

A Silent Truth

The greatest fear you could ever face is yourself.

Tevin C. R. Dubé

Would it make any sense to speak of your plans with someone who's deaf? Then why would you try to share your visions with those seeing but are ever blinded?

Always be mindful of your words. It's either you become liberated by it or incarcerated because of such.

Tevin C. R. Dubé

I have to admit, I've seen the blessings of the Most High throughout this extended period of lows in my life thus far. My sincerest request is to be more abundantly present with me throughout the many blessings and successes that you are about to bestow upon me. Amen.

A Silent Truth

I was thinking the luxury most of us have many truly don't appreciate. For instance, think how hard it must be for someone who just recently found out that they have final stage cancer and has no choice but to face the inevitability of having to die soon. Some of us may never truly know how or when we are going to exit this world but remember such is never a luxury unto the many who would appreciate the fact of not knowing.

Tevin C. R. Dubé

This might be old but never try to get back at those who never saw your worth. Just know that when you finally found the one who sees you for you, they would be looking. Your happiness will slowly eat away at them because the 'what if' and the regrets are the toughest challenges anyone has to face. Be joyful when you see others depart from you to be in search of the same thing they had already found.

A Silent Truth

Sacrifice will always come before success arrive. A dictionary too will prove this fact to be true.

Tevin C. R. Dubé

Many people are unaware of the fact that the most dangerous species it has is not a lion, or a bear, neither a hippo nor a rhino but that of a mosquito. It has the highest mortality rate every single year towards humanity. Sometimes we tend to overlook the simplest things that can quickly be multiplied unto our sudden destruction.

A Silent Truth

It is all an illusion, an apparition, a gimmick. We call it Life, we call it being human. The human experience is an overall expression of the soul but death is liberation to an imprisoned spirit.

Tevin C. R. Dubé

If you really
want to see
magic at its
finest. Reach
to the closest
mirror and take
a deep good
look within.

 simple way to understand your true strength is when it takes an entire group of people to try and just bring you bring.

Tevin C. R. Dubé

After the Most Divine One has revealed the hidden agendas of many before your foresight, it has a funny way of revealing their ugliness before their own faces. By choosing to be still and humble, at the right time the right words will be upon your tongue. And because of their pride, the Most High will use the same ones to give to you all the things they themselves were trying to withhold from you. Trust the process, as it unfolds, your eyes will be filled with amazement and astonishment.

If I'm always punctual at work, why worry when the late comers seek exaltation for their once-in-a-blue-moon accomplishments. Consistency will always outlive and outshine the brightest beams of inconsistencies. Success is not haphazard, it is a dedicated habit. It doesn't need any form of validation. It is a matter of getting the job done utilizing every obstacle as a step higher.

Tevin C. R. Dubé

When you truly set yourself to thoroughly accomplish your dreams, your determination will surely match heavenly proportions as you begin to materialise your visions into the reality you have first reconstructed within the heavens of your mind.

A Silent Truth

Listen closely to how people speak about others. The majority of the time, they paint their perceptions upon another. What do they think and say about another is exactly the same way and things they perceive others have towards them because they are the very ones who are trying to hide the same characteristics about themselves behind the veils of their sanctimonious ways and their ignorant truths about justice. You could never justify what is right for another until you have deemed it is right for yourself. This is what it means to be careful of your tongue because you are your own condemnation as much as you are your liberation.

Tevin C. R. Dubé

Have you ever heard of the phrase, "I could make them out in mud." Well, they always say a liar has no memory. Some people could keep up well with their words but the difference maker lies in their actions. A charade is but an act that has its expiration date. As the sun begins to rise in your day, it exposes another's night. Hence you can make them out even if their identities are hidden in mud because the inconsistency of their ways remain prevalent.

A Silent Truth

If youth is
beauty and
being full of
age is beauty also,
then who in
this world is
truly physically
ugly?

Tevin C. R. Dubé

There comes a time when the man who is saying peace and love are put to the test. Then there comes a time when the man who is saying revenge and war is put to the test. And then there comes a time when even the quiet and humble man must at times be put to the test and is made to cry out. Rest assured, there is a reward to be had individually.

There is true and pure glory to be inherited from a hard life that was undeservingly deserving unto you. I can talk because Experience is my tutor.

Not because I had a hard life means that I prefer a hard life for others. Not because your life wasn't as difficult as mine should give you an excuse to overlook my endeavours. My circumstances have proven to be unfortunately fortunate whereas another's life may have been proven to be a fortunately unfortunate circumstances.

straight path isn't always straight and a twisted path isn't always bend. Sometimes the right path is led the wrong way and the wrong path is led unto the right. Allow your intuition to be your guide, it is the only light you'll ever need.

Tevin C. R. Dubé

I'm not into most manmade celebrations neither am I against it but I do love to celebrate myself through the Knowledge of Self. But why are we being destroyed for acknowledging ourselves?

Believe in yourself so much that making the impossible to become possible is only second-nature. You must always strive to be the first of your kind. Learn to become a natural wonder of the world by becoming a precious gem to the entire Universe. All it takes is for you to believe in you because you are already everything you need and more.

Tevin C. R. Dubé

The more you lose only means higher the number of times you are to be counted as a winner.

A Silent Truth

The ills of the world are contagious. Many of us have been wronged, in which we have wronged others, which makes all of us wrong. We must never forget that the other side of love is to be able to endure through long sufferings. How else could Love be proven valid? An antidote could never be considered a cure without a disease present.

Tevin C. R. Dubé

If you learn from the best you may become better to help further enlighten the rest. One concept I've learned from Moses, is that you can perform miracles, hey you can even make manna fall from the sky like rain and the same people who were witnesses and fed from it will still murmur behind your back, conspire against you and after tasting freedom can still willingly choose to want to be a slave. I never choose to be a leader, that's your sight if you see me as one but I never saw that of myself. I just got up.

Death has nothing to do with the real you, it has everything to do with the body.

Tevin C. R. Dubé

The true concept of it being easier for a camel to enter through a needle's eye than it is for a rich man to enter through the gates of heaven is simple. Attachment! The Eye of the needle is the Pineal Gateway into the pure reality of heavenly spirituality. Being too attached to the physical and all of your material possessions which even includes your family and your own body are weights unto a free spirit. This is why death has become so difficult a task unto many who are dying. It is the complete acceptance to free yourself of all things physically to permanently own all things. Hence, the mystery of death is only revealed unto the ones dying. It

A Silent Truth

is the silent and absolute truth

that must be seen by the blind,

heard by the deaf and spoken

with a silent tongue. It is the

ultimate gift but only for those

with eyes to see and the

ears to hear.

Tevin C. R. Dubé

Out of all the things in the world, don't choose to be an ass. God already created such a thing.

Learn how to be happy with just the right amount. Sometimes being too happy makes others unhappy.

Tevin C. R. Dubé

If the fact remains that a lie must be told to save a life in imminent danger, how much of a lie it truly is? Would you still consider yourself a liar, even though you are lying to preserve the truth? In acute cases, a lie can be truly positive because it reflects a softer nature to the many harsh angles of the truth. The Truth loves being naked but a good lie is sometimes a cherished garment.

A Silent Truth

About a couple of months before my uncle had passed away right before his family and, we had a conversation. Him: "I could have done more to help you all out after alyuh fadda die." I interrupted him saying, "But you have done the most. So don't say that. You had no choice but to do what you had to do because if you did take me to live with you, I might have done good but you would have interrupted me from my true destiny. I may have done well in school but I would have never topped it. Uncle, you did exactly what you had to do and it was good, so don't say you could have done more when you already did the most." The moral is, we can't spoil God's Plan. Humans can see but are yet still the most blinded creatures to have ever existed up until this point thus far.

Tevin C. R. Dubé

Sometimes we are too caught up in ourselves. You must always show off all the good things in your life, in your house, about your associates and it's always about you. There is no wrong in celebrating your triumphs but it is at those moments you could be confronted with sudden defeats from within. Be mindful always. Never become too self-absorbed but opt to become absorbed by the consciousness of Self.

A Silent Truth

Jealousy is like cancer cells which everyone has within their individual body. Some just nourishes it with the right supplements by feeding their minds the wrong nutrition. And all of a sudden, you have a stage 4 diagnosis. By that time, it has already become somewhat irreversible.

Tevin C. R. Dubé

Sometimes we believe that the easiest thing to do is flee from the presence of the enemy when their power is overwhelmingly strong. Running away at times only makes them to pursue you even more. Sometimes we must trust that untamed Force that at times Nature itself seems to lose control. How else could the Holy One prepare a table for you before the presence of your enemies if you are not present for your own divine promotion?

A Silent Truth

A true friend to me is the fruits on a tree. They strive to reach to the peak of their perfection to willingly become a sacrifice. As much as I enjoy the gift of their nourishment, they enjoy the process in which it takes to finally, become one with a human.

Tevin C. R. Dubé

Never have I, neither would I ever wish physical blindness upon myself but many times before, I have wished to never be able to see.

A Silent Truth

Allow me to profoundly contradict your thoughts in the right way wrongfully and in the wrong way rightfully. Allow me to show you the right way wrongly and the wrong way rightly so.

Tevin C. R. Dubé

The human is a true friend to the Earth, the Earth is a true friend to Nature, Nature is a true friend to the Universe, the Universe is a true friend to The Great Beyond, The Great Beyond is a true friend to the eternal All in All, and the eternal All in All is a great friend to Infinity-Infinitely, and Infinity-Infinitely is a great friend to the undetectable presence of Absolute Existence Itself. Only a carnal mind is unable to fathom and see the complete infusion of the Spirit because it seems and feels to be separate because of the cubicle spacing of its little boxlike mindset. Even Existence exists within itself. In the same way, there are many seas of men as semen within a man there is an infinite supply

A Silent Truth

of eggs within a single female. Just
as much as every seed has a tree
within with many seeds and with each
seed a tree and so on infinitely.
Existence exists within itself.

Tevin C. R. Dubé

Learn to be humble, learn to be by yourself. Then watch yourself be exalted mysteriously and see how much all the right people will be rushing to stand firmly by your side.

A Silent Truth

When the sun is too hot people complain about the drought and dryness. When there is heavy rainfall, people complain about the flood and mud. Some are totally in love with the sun and others with the rain. Nature continues to perpetuate its actions disregarding the fact that it is no easy task to please mortals but with the genuine intention to teach pure balance. After all, Nature has all the time in the world. During extreme heat, prepare for the rain by creating large cisterns and solid walkways. As a result of such, during the drought, you will never thirst or be without food and during the heavy downpours, your feet shall never become muddy. After such, no one will be one-sided and a biased lover of the same element that takes on the appearance of many.

Tevin C. R. Dubé

I does try my best to
make everyone feel
at home anywhere
because I do freely
open up the doors to
a heart filled with
compassion. I keep
showing it even
though it is rarely and
genuinely given back
in return.

The most dangerous thing in life is to play it safe.

Tevin C. R. Dubé

Sometimes the hurdles in Life seems to be a Mount Everest climb but as long as you make it across, you would have learned an unknown truth about yourself.

Always remember a new destination would always seem to be longer than expected due to the unfamiliarity of the route. Be patient and enjoy every moment of journey.

Tevin C. R. Dubé

Aye, I feel like shouting. There will be so many highlights in my life to come that all my troubles will miserably fade out of existence for good. I have seen it. I am going to be fat with a great abundance of all the magnificent things my heart had ever desired. And yet greater things beyond my lucid dreams and vivid imaginations shall be freely bestowed to provoke a further sense of profound astonishment. Asé.

A Silent Truth

People are always looking for something or someone else to believe in but can barely find the time to search for and believe in themselves.

Tevin C. R. Dubé

The more I feel like things are coming to an end or whenever I feel like giving up the most, the impetus from a divine inspiration keeps on proving to me that the Holy Supreme isn't finished with me just yet. I am reminded that I am not going anywhere soon because I heard it from a Great Voice that speaks A Silent Truth.

A Silent Truth

aving some struggles is not the true problem. It is a most dangerous period when none no longer exist.

Tevin C. R. Dubé

The easy road is problematic towards self-growth. Sugar is sweet but bitter as diabetes.

A Silent Truth

s a man in today's stereotypical society, I am strong enough to tell anyone that I care about them and that I love them.

Tevin C. R. Dubé

Isn't it better when you have to work hard for what you want? That way, you have little choice but to appreciate the many great things you have in your life. Whenever things are inherited too easily, there is a tendency for it to be mistreated and taken for granted. Irresponsibility will make you lose everything. All things are good but the greatest things never come easy.

A Silent Truth

There is some truth in the saying that the sky is the limit. But since I know that there is no such thing as a sky, then I am shooting to accomplish all my dreams with endless possibilities and zero limitations.

Tevin C. R. Dubé

B efore I lose
you don't let
me lose you.

A Silent Truth

The sky isn't the limit. I Am my own limit and guess what, I found out that I Am of a limitless Nature and I Am unlimited because of Nature because I Am Nature's unlimited programming.

Tevin C. R. Dubé

We all deserve the best but not too many are willing to earn it.

A Silent Truth

The pigmented man as a whole is a threat. An educated pigmented man as a whole is an even bigger threat. An educated pigmented man that holds a pen as a whole is even a greater threat. But the greatest threat that exists is an educated pigmented man holding a pen that is fully awakened as a whole. Knowledge of Self was never an Earthly threat, it is a perpetual Universal Movement.

Tevin C. R. Dubé

Sometimes it takes distance to get close. Sometimes it takes separation to attain togetherness. There is positivity to be found amidst negativity as much as there is a balanced amount of negativity to be had amidst positivity.

A Silent Truth

The same way sugar easily dissolves in hot water, allow your struggles to be easily diffused into your life path. You may get sweetened in the process.

Tevin C. R. Dubé

A sponge once free from all moisture after being saturated is no longer the same ever again. Even if it was ever to get dry again it never dries the same. It becomes brittle and quickly deteriorates. It must now be constantly soaked for longevity. Self makes the body search for the soul, the soul then seeks the spirit, and the spirit then seeks to become One with The All. Knowledge of Self is a pure conscious state of continuous evolution through Absolute Freedom. After that first sip, only eternity could quench such an intended thirst.

A Silent Truth

Life sees and knows your genuine desires. It also knows that on our own, most of us are unable to find our bearings unto the many great things we truly deserve because of our comfort zones and our quick ability to settle. So many times we are given the push we deserve, unfortunately for us, we see it as trials and not opportunities.

Tevin C. R. Dubé

I don't ever see myself as someone reaching for the stars. I see myself already being that star which is simply on course towards a destination that was perfectly designed just for me.

Many truly believe that they could have stopped me but the redness in their eyes blinded them from seeing that I Am a Green Light. I Am the Universal confidence of gamma rays second to myself already being the very Big Bang of physical existence, manifesting pure spirituality.

Tevin C. R. Dubé

It's good to not
rush into
anything
especially a
relationship.

A Silent Truth

If I cannot see myself living with someone then I would never opt to date them if I had a chance. Why choose to live a lie because of an uncertain mind? Why choose to hurt that person but more yourself during that process of selfish pursuits. Be open from the start, let two-way communication be your initial foundation and save both yourselves from a sleeping world with unknown troubles.

Tevin C. R. Dubé

Dreams are the foresight of a sleeping body but visions are the foresight of an awakened soul.

Everything in
Life takes time.
Even time
takes time for
everything else
to be on time.

Tevin C. R. Dubé

If we take note of a simple book laid out in its simplicity, we would all have the greatest lives possible. Imagine a bunch of one, two, three, four and five letter words coming together to formulate an entire book.

A Silent Truth

When you're in peace just note that you have everything to lose and even though war has loses and casualties, you still have a lot to gain.

Tevin C. R. Dubé

When you become aligned with Nature's Order you would soon realise that you are never truly under the weather. You are only going through the different phases by learning to create the path that perfectly connects it all. It is the establishment of spiritual balance physically.

Being a couple is not about being perfect and always agreeing with each other. Being a couple simply means that each is on a separate journey in Life with each being dedicated to help one another to endure their task until it ends. It is to bring comfort and have understanding when no one else can't. Today it can solely be based upon sex.

Tevin C. R. Dubé

Sometimes we tell ourselves that a door has been closed off from us when in reality, it was never opened in the first place.

A Silent Truth

The more you quiet the tongue and humble the soul, the louder you hear the silent truth of a more unnaturally natural tone.

Tevin C. R. Dubé

I never thought it would be you. I never thought I would be a hidden gem of the Universe. An endless treasure hidden amongst men abiding within the flesh.

A Silent Truth

I see people

trying to withhold

a yard of cloth

from me but

unknowingly

leading me

towards

inheriting bolts of

different fabrics.

Tevin C. R. Dubé

They say no one man is an island. That maybe true for others but I Am the containment of an entire Universe.

A Silent Truth

Sometimes you must be plucked out from your immediate surroundings and be transplanted within another. It doesn't mean that you would not have survived there but you would have never been able to truly grow towards your fullest potential. You may have been a flower being stunned within a little pot but if replanted into an open garden then you would be able to bloom in all your splendour.

Tevin C. R. Dubé

If you keep finding yourself to be confronted by dark situations its simply because you are the light to make a way through. Don't see yourself being confronted but rather being beseeched for help. All things dark seek the light source to be illuminated as well because not even a spot of light could be contained by the paleness of black.

Come to think of it, I haven't faced anything in Life even though I have faced a lot. Judging from my life today and my many accomplishments are proof that I was able to truly see and capitalise upon the many opportunities for self-growth that was given.

Tevin C. R. Dubé

The true story of success has never lied in the end results but entirely rests upon the determination one has inherited while enduring and persevering throughout humble beginnings. The latter represents the qualities of already being successful whereas the results are just proof of a success already attained.

Money and power could never truly convert a man, it just unleashes hidden traits that didn't have the need to be revealed just yet because the platform wasn't right.

Tevin C. R. Dubé

All natural foods and fruits are as a result of a blooming flower. Allow yourself to be naturally pollinated and as you begin to bloom other's will eventually acknowledge the flower that has been blooming to bear good fruits all along.

A Silent Truth

Learn to be a trendsetter, learn to defy all odds. Learn to be like the letter "I" in a sentence. Whenever it's by Itself, it remains capital at the Alpha the Omega and even in between.

Tevin C. R. Dubé

I love to see myself as dirt. It may not seem like much but all natural resources and manmade creations came from and are as a result of it. So yeah, I'm intricately designed and highly fashionable but do appear with great simplicity.

A Silent Truth

I could see the
light in my
darkest night
and the darkness
in my brightest day.
I am afraid and
yet still I am brave,
such is the nature
of new experiences.

Tevin C. R. Dubé

Negative people are like a silent leakage of water below the Earth. They cut and undermine you slowly and then all of a sudden, a landslip appears out of nowhere to take everything down. Isn't it a better thing to see the problem beforehand so that you could build upon solid grounds? This is why we must never choose to get upset when negative people are silently being exposed before our faces. Isn't it better to see the threat first so that they would never be able to undermine and suddenly destroy in one day all the things which took years to be established? Many times we see our greatest blessings as curses.

I could never force
anyone to conform
unto me or my
principles. That would
be selfish but if I'm to
prove myself
selflessly interested, I
would learn how to
blend into their
personality through a
cognitive
overstanding.

Tevin C. R. Dubé

The wind does blow rough at times, the Earth shakes beneath my feet. I've slipped before, fell many times, been the object of rejection, suppression and oppression but yet still, I was silently taught how to be strong and now being strong is all I know.

ll days are beautiful. If it's raining use it as an opportunity to store some of its joy in order to amplify the beauty of a sunny day after becoming saturated.

Tevin C. R. Dubé

Sometimes we are the very ones who are destroying the very good things in our lives. And then when things are not going our way we ask for deliverance and don't know what we are truly asking for. Sometimes we keep going through it without even realising that if your situation were to be permanently solved, it would involve the permanent removal of yourself in more ways than one. How great it is that most times we are being spared from ourselves?

A Silent Truth

heart pure of
gold passes
through the tests
of fire to be
purified. Our pains
is that fire. It
won't last forever
but our healing is
the jewels crafted
to perfection.

Tevin C. R. Dubé

What matters greatly is the fact that you've tried. The what if factor in Life can be unbearable especially when you regret the fact that you never made an attempt at pursuing your dreams and life goals. It's hard not knowing how the turn of events could have been. In the same way, things can go sour it can be sweet. Don't be afraid of failure because failure is the pathway leading to success.

A Silent Truth

What I've learnt from this Life is that opportunities do too revolve in a cycle. Once you've missed yours from being too preoccupied with solely focusing on things you want, you become blinded by things you need. As you preoccupy yourself with miscellaneous things, you lose sight of the miracles and breakthroughs that were presented before your face. As the wheel spins, your turn has to rotate once more and it becomes harder and harder as the things you 'want' so badly always seems to fall apart.

Tevin C. R. Dubé

Human love is a far cry from what is real love. The strength of Love is never tested by a broken heart but through the emotions that flow through it. If your love isn't tested, how else could you ever learn to love for real? You begin to appreciate the simplest acts of kindness and consideration because you truly understand what it means to give. But you can also identify the same within another who is in a similar place to you mentally. No one is looking forward to anything but still has everything else to give. Such a mutuality is when two broken pieces were intentionally broken through the tests of love to be a complete fit for each other. This type of love is amazing and unbreakable.

A Silent Truth

Humility is when the day is already about you but you take some of that time to make it about many significant others.

Tevin C. R. Dubé

Today is Albert Einstein's birthday. Today Stephen Hawking passed away. But today is the beginning of a new era for Tevin Dubé who has solved the many mysteries that have long eluded their minds. Talk about cosmic alignment. Today also marks a day with my Life Path. 14/3/2018

A Silent Truth

Let me explain what fight down is truly about. A person who admires someone's long hair but when another begins to grow theirs, they jest against the beginning stages of their endeavours.

Tevin C. R. Dubé

I now move forward throughout Existence as a human being through the expressions of Life and Decay. To be and not to be. I Am the spirit that dwells amidst a consciousness so pure.

A Silent Truth

You want to know what is amazing to me? In a place where many are struggling, instead of helping each other to be comfortable, there are still those who aspire to be the richest poor.

Tevin C. R. Dubé

In a nation of a 100 people, if 99 are thoroughly happy and 1 is thoroughly unhappy, then that nation level of happiness is measured by the unhappiness of that 1 person.

A Silent Truth

They say leave
room for
disappointment
but little do
they know that
room is
expectation.

Tevin C. R. Dubé

One thing about me, I don't fall in love. But that doesn't make approve of me being incapable of showing genuine love. It's just that I've been to a place where my genuine nature was taken advantage of for me to save my most precious resources for those who truly deserve the very best. Myself! I'll forever be shrouded in mystery to the entire world because the secret to me was never intended to be revealed to everyone. Only a small percentage. Only someone of a rare nature shall inherit the rarity of me.

I'm at a place
where there is
no second guessing
or double-mindedness.
Either it is or
it isn't.

Tevin C. R. Dubé

I remember it was just a little less than a couple of weeks ago I reached a major breaking point. I was beginning to lose all hope as I no longer wanted to care for anyone. There was no longer anything that could anchor my spirit from floating away. But all of a sudden the grace of a Force Divine intervened on my behalf and presented a solution to my void. My silent prayers are being answered and I'm forever grateful that my eyes were able to see it. A spark can shine as bright as the sun in the midst of an impenetrable darkness. I found an anchor to help keep me grounded from not floating away forever just yet.

The deepest
oceans can be
turbulent atop
while still being
calm deep
beneath.

Tevin C. R. Dubé

I guess God created everything because of loneliness but even though being surrounded by everything still choose to remain alone. I guess this is what God feels like. A disconnected connection.

A Silent Truth

No matter how powerful or influential you are you have no such thing towards someone who doesn't require the need for it.

Tevin C. R. Dubé

It's so strange that you'll give the world to everyone and to no one you don't even mean as much as an island far more for the world. That's how I'm feeling at the moment but say what, keep it moving, such is Life.

I work best under oppression, rejection and suppression. I make myself the best out of these not-so-best situations. It's a bitter-sweet life I've been living all my life.

I guess when
you no longer
look forward to
anything except
for what you
rightfully deserve
that's when you
have everything
to give.

It's not you. It's just not you. Acceptance is a beautiful thing. It is you, it is you. Acceptance is a beautiful thing.

Tevin C. R. Dubé

Hello Darkness my old friend. It's the deafening silence that connects me and you time and again.

A Silent Truth

Just watch me relax as I put in this work overtime.

Tevin C. R. Dubé

The conception of light happened in the midst of darkness. Some people only love to dwell in the light. I decided to penetrate the dark and the feeling of it is sweeter than sex at its climax.

A Silent Truth

I have become so in tune with my subconscious mind, that before I do anything, I must consult with it. My writings/quotes are initially heard from deep within before I state them. I've become familiar with the unknown, I've been to Nowhere many times. I keep hearing loudly that voiceless voice. I've become One with Nothing itself. An emotionally emotionless connection was made. I might appear to be quite human before your face. A desert-like appearance to many but in reality an oasis that appears commonplace.

Tevin C. R. Dubé

My sighs are more frequent and getting quite heavy. Feels like I'm being tested more by death than mere tiredness.

lways
remember
don't nobody
want you unless
they need you or
can use you.

Tevin C. R. Dubé

Two options when you are buried:
1. Remain dead.
2. Rise like a seed in germination.

A Silent Truth

Even the Almighty Most High Divine moves in silence. Don't get mad with the pupil who follow the instructions effectively.

Tevin C. R. Dubé

Sometimes the best thing that ever happened to us was the worst.

A Silent Truth

Lesson learnt. It's always the ones closest to you who tries to sabotage your growth. In a world filled with people and I still have to remain alone. The thought alone is most depressing and uplifting at the same time.

Tevin C. R. Dubé

I think that the
things that you
are destined to
receive presents
itself to you
long before you
inherit it.

A Silent Truth

I'm at a point where I allow the process to take place naturally. I'm not rushing it neither am I trying to hold it back. If it's to be then it will be and if it's not to be then it will be as well.

Tevin C. R. Dubé

So many trust issues in the world. No one wants to believe another but wants everyone to believe them when they say that they are being honest.

A Silent Truth

Stop feeling sorry for the people who have died and how they have died. It may not be under the best circumstances from time to time neither are some acceptable or even worthy but it doesn't change the fact that we all got to leave the flesh. Feel sorry for yourself and those still alive because we may witness others' departure but somebody will live to witness ours. But until then you do not know the day, the time or the hour for you.

Tevin C. R. Dubé

I am a giver and not a taker. I do just keep on giving. When I run out of the physical, it's always the mental and emotional and the spiritual I'm giving. It is exhausting and depleting and enervating. I guess I am strong enough to endure it but honestly, I does try my best to stop but I can't and that's also a major the reason why I would rather be by myself and be cut off from it all. It seems like all efforts are destined to be successfully failed attempts in the end.

A Silent Truth

How can something be sweet and sour at the same time but with great savour? Yes I am that bitter-sweet savoury tasting tamarind ball.

Tevin C. R. Dubé

Even an imitation brings a sense of hope to those who are unable to gain an original. I would always respect the temporal joys you brought to me while the original was saying that I was way out of its league. And when I reach into and beyond the leagues of the original state, I'll enshrine the steps of the authentic imitation before all.

A Silent Truth

The imitations had been my true friends all my life and I dare not switch up on them amongst the so-called originals. A misfit that was deliberately cut badly with the intention to never fit in.

Tevin C. R. Dubé

I am a writer and I hate writing now. I wish I had a switch for my brain to take it on and off at will. Too many thoughts to execute with so little time to do It, with no real opportunities given and so many burdens on my mind. It's only one me Lord and I don't want to self-destruct in the process. To whom much is given much is tested and I didn't ask for all this load.

A Silent Truth

The greatest and hardest thing to practice in life is love. The greatest feeling still to attain is being numb. Well, I've mastered both. I'm lovingly numbed.

Tevin C. R. Dubé

In my mind there are so many beautiful things that I have and is yet still to create. No wonder why I prefer to dream in there while I'm awake in this nightmare.

A Silent Truth

K eep looking for all my flaws and watch me attain perfection.

Tevin C. R. Dubé

The heart wants what it wants. Sometimes you have to step back and stop making everyone else feel wanted and see how much of a priority you are in other people's life. Trust me I've seen my true worth and where I stand currently. I can identify the doves of hope in my low times just in order for me to make out the pigeons that'll be flocking around to peck at the bread baked for me. All pretenders have and are still being exposed in the little time I'd chosen to be alone. Lesson learned and a great blessing earned.

The anti-venom is made with and from the venom itself. Remember that the cure to all problems lie with and within the problem itself.

Tevin C. R. Dubé

New Beginnings would always be hard when you keep holding on to old Endings.

A Silent Truth

The sweetest songs come from an instrument that is constantly played and used. A brand-new equipment always needs tuning. Sometimes in Life we feel the same way, used, misused and abused. We feel like giving in and giving up for good but remember the sweetest music comes from a regularly already used instrument. We are Life's instruments being tuned and used to sing symphonies of various songs.

I guess when I start lying you'll see the truth.

A Silent Truth

If I could learn to do
all this on my own
then surely I'll learn to
enjoy it all the same.
If you never aided me
along the way don't
expect anything but
the same in return.
Where no love is lost
there is no love to be
found there.

Tevin C. R. Dubé

It is a blessing to differentiate between illusion and reality. It is a blessing to know when it's time to walk away. It is a blessing knowing when it is time to let go. It is a blessing when you can be at peace with accepting the facts that surround you. It is a blessing when you can finally do something without anyone hindering your growth. It is a blessing when you can still rejoice after rejection. It is a blessing when you realise the things you cared about you should've never cared about and now you no longer care about them. What a blessing such a blessing is!

A Silent Truth

I'll be looking
on from within
the shadows.
The light isn't
always
revealing but
blinding
sometimes.

Tevin C. R. Dubé

Even an unexpectedly good surprise can still bear unwanted disappointments.

A Silent Truth

People would talk so beautiful upfront and then get utterly indifferent and bitter way before the end.

Tevin C. R. Dubé

It would be a very
long bitter cold
day for those who
never ceased the
many precious
opportunities
I've presented
to them time
and again.

A Silent Truth

I've exhausted my giveaways. I kept giving and giving until I had nothing left. I've silently lost my sanity for blatant ungratefulness. I'm not looking forward to seeing you fit your foot in these shoes. I'm not a vindictive person. When I change these shoes I don't need you walking near me. You scuffed my previous ones and made a mockery of me in general while practising humanity. Now you must stand afar and watch me walk in grace as both me and the memory of you leave for good.

 simple lesson can be your biggest blessing while your biggest blessing can be your greatest lesson.

A Silent Truth

The final whistle has blown and the last bell has rung.

Tevin C. R. Dubé

I don't ever get angry. Anger is blinding. However, I do become furious because my eyes are made to see many things in advance and reveal the hidden agendas. So whenever I get furious just know that everything does be unfolding before my very eyes itself.

Anger makes you act out uncontrollably whereas to be furious requires advanced critical thinking and calculated decisions.

Tevin C. R. Dubé

The new definition for parliamentary ministers:

Each member knowing
their colleagues are
involved in racketeering,
with each trying to find out
exactly what it is, so whenever
the opportunity arises, it can
be effectively utilised
towards their own
capitalisation.

A Silent Truth

I've pulled many out of great pits and it was a great thing to do. But when I'm in mine, there is no real help to be given. To me, it feels like a group of cheerleaders. Just a bunch of acrobatics and pompoms cheering me on as I have to draw mysterious strengths to hold on as I uphold all my weight dangling from a fine thread.

Tevin C. R. Dubé

When I'm doing something, I don't do it for me, I do it to benefit all those around me. But when I see others doing something that is done solely for their benefit with little care of the fact that it is badly affecting me. I promise there will come a time when I'll be doing me with little sympathy for the misery of those. As I see Nature taking its natural course, I'll keep my mind at bay, my lips sealed and my hands restrained. I'll no longer hinder the process of anything that surrounds that environment.

A Silent Truth

I've received so many blessings but the depth of my wounds those blessings are yet to fill. Those wounds are so infected that even my blessings feel more cursed than my curses themselves. But I guess those blessings are the methylated spirits to my wounds. All the same, they both are equally painful.

Tevin C. R. Dubé

Some people only love fairytale endings as for me, I've been praying for my day-mares and nightmares to just disappear from within my soul.

A Silent Truth

To all those directly and indirectly involved in my struggles it's either you'll testify to my triumphs or you'll become the testimony about it.

Tevin C. R. Dubé

Facebook: A friendless place full of friends. Messenger: A place full of messengers but no good messages. Phone: A place full of contacts but no one contacting. Life: A place full of dead people that are claiming to be alive.

A Silent Truth

I had a dream some years back about me getting married. The same day we got married, my wife got pregnant with another man at the wedding and bearing the child at the same time. I left the ceremony torn between places. Then I heard a voice telling me that I had a choice to let love live or let love die. I contemplated deeply about it and I said I'll choose to let love live as much as I wanted to let it die. I saw a young woman appear and she was waiting on me for a while. Dreams are so encrypted and not what they seem. Moral is I have the choice to choose whatever I want, at any time. Today I am truly letting love live after all I've been through. I am still searching for that source of comfort that is awaiting me.

Tevin C. R. Dubé

I don't hope and
pray for luck.
I work hard.
Even when I'm
resting, my mind
is always contemplating
my next move.

A Silent Truth

The way my inner sight is showing me a lot, one of my main fear and triumph is that I would barely have anyone close to enjoying it all with.

Tevin C. R. Dubé

I've never loved shallow waters. You can't swim properly.

A Silent Truth

Life do give some of us salt and expect sugar. So if it expects sugar from salt and it is required from you, then give it exactly what it expects. Put that salt upon a grapefruit or a not-too sweet orange and make it taste sweet like sugar.

Tevin C. R. Dubé

Whenever you start to feel the pressures from your comfort zone surroundings, it could mean Life is fixing the wood below your fireside to make your heat become more intense and unbearable to those who trying to stifle your flames with green leaves and smoke.

A Silent Truth

You can't expect me to work and then pray for a salary I rightfully earned.

Tevin C. R. Dubé

Be careful of those who you choose to kick while they are down. They may well be a giant in disguise because of their low-state while lying down.

A Silent Truth

Today was a major turning point in my life. All I've endured was for this one moment in time. Now in just one day all my labours are being given its rightful recommendation. My short story and TV debut is already out for the entire world to see the boy who was a hidden treasure all along.

20/04/2018

Tevin C. R. Dubé

As the body contracts a virus we tend to get sick as we enter a more weakened state. It is in the same manner Life's adversities can affect us. As the body feels susceptible to the virus, it's only because the immune system is working on becoming stronger. It is in the same manner we have to continue working through the adversities of Life to strengthen our minds and conquer all odds.

A Silent Truth

I'm way in over my head with certain things, I don't even know why I bother or even try. I don't know if I love a challenge or if I'm just acting out of stupidity. Either way, I do be in over my head because I don't like to 'what if' myself. But at the same time, I don't have any more room for losing and hurt. Should I stand or should I sit, should I try or should I quit? I was brave to be brave but now I'm brave to be sacred because being scared saves me from the hurt of being too brave. I never feared rejection because I fought even though I knew I was unevenly matched. But the consistency of it prevailing over me made me respect it. I choose to be alone in loneliness and in loneliness I choose to remain alone. Even though I've grown accustomed to being hurt, I'm still afraid of continuously being hurt.

Tevin C. R. Dubé

After so many people washed their mouths on you charged you with things they have no evidence of, tarnished your name and drag it through the filth of their tongues, kept gossiping behind your back but with flattering lips and a double heart they speak before your presence, it feels great when the Most High slaps them in their faces with a blow that they are made to eat the bitter grapes of their own sowing without you having to lift up a single finger nor utter a single word to them. Progress breeds enemies but your best revenge is your success. And by such, every head shall bow and every tongue shall confess. Even your enemies shall exalt your name and profess you to be the best. Selah.

Some people dry season can be cold as a blizzard.

Tevin C. R. Dubé

Life can be so funny at times. Sometimes receiving nothing means to receive everything at that appointed time. It is hard to understand something especially when it hasn't been explained at the beginning. Such is the case with this existence. You must always walk without knowing the outcome until you reach that specific destination. You have to always bear through, holding on to the bitterness of hope for something savoury. This existence is like a job, you must work first before you get paid. This existence is like grapes, it has to be sour before it gets sweet. You must always suffer before you are comforted. It is never fully

A Silent Truth

understood at the beginning because
the explanation lies along
the journey but the full answer
lies at the end of it all. This
existence is like mathematics. You
must first work through the problem
step by step before you can arrive
at the answer that lies beneath
all the workings.

Tevin C. R. Dubé

Sometimes you may feel like you're going backwards but sometimes it is the greatest advance in moving forward.

Feel great even
though you
may not be
feeling good.

Tevin C. R. Dubé

Everyone wants to be loved by somebody but doesn't want to take the initiative to love somebody. Disclaimer fact, many wants to be loved by specific individuals with specific qualities and characteristics. Stop entertaining talk with people who are genuinely interested in you but deep down you know you are not interested in them. If that's the case, stop leading people on because you just want to feel wanted until something that fits your description comes along. Stop playing with people's emotions. And oh yes, you're not doing them any favours by not trying to make them feel bad by you trying to play it safe. You're not being nice

A Silent Truth

by not trying to make them feel low,
you're setting them up to feel
hurt more than ever. You are
psychologically murdering people.
That's why people who tend to have a
lot of choices does end up making
the wrong selection because they have
become cursed by it.

Tevin C. R. Dubé

A title that is inherited from men by men can be easily taken away because they have the power to strip you of such as it is a manmade creation. But to the things that are inherited naturally are a blessing from Nature. Nature is eternal. Not even Death could relinquish you from it. For example, Marcus Garvey Jr., Malcolm X, Martin Luther King Jr., Nelson Mandela, Bob Marley, Patrick Manning and the newest inductee, Tevin Dubé.

A Silent Truth

A lot of people fail to see that all prophets before were never perfect even though they are perfect. This is so because many of us who are perfect, fail to realise such due to our imperfections. Life places situations in our lives not merely for our development but really for us to remember and establish the perfection of our true nature. Many of us tend to forget about it as we go through our overall human experience. It is through our imperfections we are made perfect. The situations in which we are confronted by or have become a victim to is to serve as a reminder to remember the realness of a compassionate nature we already possess but had temporally failed to remember because such is the nature of being human.

Tevin C. R. Dubé

The realisation of this existence is to first understand that you are not perfect just to realise how much of a perfect being you really are. Only someone who's perfect reiterates the fact that they are not perfect. Humility in itself is that of perfection itself.

A Silent Truth

Imagination is truly

a great thing

but when backed

by belief and

a sheer determination

and dedication

towards hard work,

it results in true

Creation.

Tevin C. R. Dubé

If Life was supposed to strip everyone of all their money and the things money can buy, I wonder how many of us would have anything of real value?

Nature is an uncovered womb. A place where you get to witness the procreation of Life in all its splendour. Life and Death are both expressions of each other. Life is an infinite pathway being led unto Death. Whereas, Death is the doorway that transitions Life unto a pathway of an eternal existence infinitely.

Tevin C. R. Dubé

Every mango tree produces some forced ripe mangoes. However, it's only a matter of time before they prematurely fall off. Drake had to cut off his then-girlfriend not that he didn't love her but due to her inability to see and support his dream of becoming a mega pop star. Megan Markle had to make a tough decision to split from her previous marriage but in time to find love within the British Monarchy. She still became a Duchess despite the fact of breaking fundamental royal protocols. Sometimes the greatest decisions in Life can also be the toughest ones. True self-love can require you to cut off your right hand, for it is better to enter into the mind state of heaven a maim and be restored than to perish the whole body because of one bad limb.

A Silent Truth

The more you try to prove your worth to others, the less valuable you become.

Tevin C. R. Dubé

I realised that there was no way for me, so I created one. That's the true difficulty that is faced in this pursuit of happiness. There are new problems unique to you that no one has ever yet faced because no one has ever truly been on the path you're on because that path has never yet existed. Others will praise you for your trailblazing mindset because you would have made it a lot easier for many to walk to places they thought were out of reach and never even knew that they have existed before.

Anyone can give you advice but not everyone can advise you.

Tevin C. R. Dubé

In Trinidad the Chinese are famous for their restaurants, groceries and the establishment of the Chinese Association. The Caucasians are famous for their fast food chain outlets. The Syrians are famous for their major business ventures. The Indians are famous for the love of land, agriculture and the establishment of the Maha Sabha. Many of the so-called 'Africans' are famous for still being mentally enslaved.

A Silent Truth

As a dark-skinned youth in this Life, if you don't get up and make your moves, you would never be successful. Almost everything and everyone is against us.

www.ingramcontent.com/pod-product-compliance
Lightning Source LLC
Chambersburg PA
CBHW071258110426
42743CB00042B/1085